CELTIC BORDERS

Aidan Meehan was born in 1951 in Northern Ireland,
and educated in Newry and at Queen's University, Belfast.
After leaving Ireland in 1973, he discovered a deep interest in Celtic art,
which led to his eight-volume *Celtic Design Series* and to his
Celtic Patterns Painting Book and *Celtic Alphabets*,
also published by Thames and Hudson.

CELTIC BORDERS

Aidan Meehan

With 244 illustrations

Thames and Hudson

artwork and typography
copyright © 1999 Aidan Meehan

British Library Cataloguing-in-Publication Data
A catalogue record for this book is
available from the British Library

ISBN 0-500-28067-3

Printed and bound in Spain

Contents

INTRODUCTION

The Purpose of This Book

The purpose of this book is to provide useful
models on which you can draw to design your
own Celtic borders. These borders are not
intended to be used as clip art. They are
original designs, created specially in order to
show a number of approaches to filling the
same layout, so that by studying the model of
your choice, you will be inspired to create
your own designs. I will discuss various
aspects of each border so that you may get a
better idea of what kind of considerations must
be taken into account if a Celtic border design
is to be successful as such. Though the designs
are all my own work, the approach I have taken
is absolutely traditional.

If you like you may use my plans as a basis for your own ideas, or as a practical exercise if you are interested in studying the methods and techniques involved in designing Celtic borders. It is not easy to make a Celtic border, unless you have many models to choose from. In the tradition, there are a great many constants which must be observed, but it is not easy to identify these standards from the sources available, there are so few. Those that have come down to us are often too incredibly elaborate to be of much practical use. And I know of no single source that presents a complete range of Celtic ornamental borders in a form simple and consistent enough to be explored as a course of study in itself. Yet this is what is required of the student who sets out to create a Celtic border. In these twenty borders I have adopted a consistent, standard layout and applied Celtic designs to it, and so I hope that it will be easier to identify the principles involved, and that as a result we may hope to see a resurgence of invention and creativity in this field, rather than the repetition of stock samples from worn-out clip-art collections.

In this introduction, I would like to tell you how I went about making the borders for this book, what materials I found useful, and the various stages that need to be completed in the process. A lot of borders did not make it into the final collection, as the plan I finally adopted did not suddenly come to me. The preliminary borders had to be abandoned, and later, successive variations had to be curtailed. Step and maze patterns, I ignored as too easy, and knots and spirals, I skipped over, as each would too easily fill a whole book in itself. For the rest, animal and plant motifs, these are by far the favourite border elements of the old painters and carvers, and for me, they offer the most variety and interest. They are also the least often attempted, as being just too difficult, compared to the more simple, purely mathematical patterns. They are all the more intriguing for that. Hopefully, by the time you finish reading this book, you will be able to read the conventions that underlie Celtic borders, and, even if you do not have the interest or compulsion to try your own hand at it, you will be better able to appreciate the great artistry of the old masters, whose borders carved in rock and painted on pages still delight us, more today than ever before.

HOW THESE BORDERS WERE MADE
Materials
First of all, you will need a sketchbook, tracing paper, low-tack adhesive tape, pencil and

eraser, drawing pen and ink. These are usually available at your local artists' supply store. The bigger suppliers often have mail-order catalogues too, if you prefer.

The Artists' Sketchbook
Sketchbooks come in all shapes and sizes, but you will need one that is at least a standard letter size. The standard letter size, 8 ½" x 11", is the size that paper comes ready cut for personal printers and photocopy machines. It also happens to be the size of the pages in this book. The classic artists' sketchbook is stitchbound in a hard cover, which allows it to lie flat when open, and protects it for a long time. Ideally, get one with paper made from rag rather than from wood pulp. Wood pulp contains acid which slowly burns the paper so that it will turn yellow with age. Newsprint, for example, is made from wood pulp, and will not last more than a few years. It is sold in pads that look like sketchpads, but is not meant for artwork, only as a handy surface of ink-free paper. Rag paper is acid free. You should only use acid-free paper.

Tracing Paper
Tracing paper should also be acid free. That is because the tracing we shall be doing is the sort you will want to keep, for these tracings

may be reused. Border designs are modular: you can retrace one design onto a different layout, expand or contract it, adapt one tracing it to different proportions, as for instance to produce a matching set of letterhead, envelope, notecard or calling card. Many hours' work go into the tracing, and you will want to mount it into your sketchbook after you have done with it, between two clean, blank sheets, so that it will not smudge or transfer onto another drawing.

Tracing paper comes in pads or rolls, and the roll is more economic. Acid-free tracing paper is made for professionals, and is worth stocking up. A roll not only lasts longer, but is more versatile, as it is not limited to one format like the pad. However, if you do get a pad just to trace these borders, get one at least A4 size.

Geometrical Instruments
For laying out the borders, some geometrical instruments may be helpful, such as a ruler, a right-angle triangle or set-square, a pair of compasses and a pair of dividers.

THE GRID
Drawing the Grid
The grid we shall use is based on a page that is eight and a half inches wide by eleven inches

long. That is, a standard letter-sized page. I
have made all these border designs to fit this
same size, allowing a half inch of empty margin
all round, which makes room to tape down the
edges of the tracing paper beyond the edge of
the border. You will need to draw up a grid
for a full page, allow a half inch all round, and
divide the rest into squares so that each square
is one and a quarter inches, or the width of our
borders. Make a master grid, as perfectly
square and exact as you can make it. Trace off
this grid, transferring the intersection points
as little crosses for the corners of the squares,
and you will find this very helpful in ensuring
that the repeating patterns fit neatly into the
borders.

THE MARKING CARD
To lay out the grid, I used a marking card to
transfer measurements to the page. The
marking card is a two inch square of card with
a unit measurement of half an inch marked on
one side of the square, and a second unit of an
inch and a quarter marked on another side. The
measures are then transferred from the card to
the paper, so that we are using exactly the same
units throughout.

Starting from the lower right-hand corner of
the page, mark a point half an inch from the

edge, and half an inch in from the right-hand edge. This will be the starting point of the rectangle.

Move a few inches up the right-hand edge of the paper, and mark a second point half an inch in. Repeat another few inches up the side. Three guide marks are enough to place the line accurately.

Join the three guide marks with a pencil line. This line will define the right-hand edge of the rectangle grid. Make the line more than ten inches long. Check that the line passes through the three marks. If it is not exact, the rest of the grid will be off also. It is better to erase the line at this stage, and redo it so that it is as exact as you can manage. Since you can never trust that the paper is cut perfectly square, you should use a right-angled triangle to set off the lower edge of the rectangle. Place a right-angled triangle with its square corner against the starting point for the rectangle, which you will have established as just described, half an inch up from the bottom of the page and half an inch in from the right-hand edge. If your triangle is large enough, use it to draw the line. If it is smaller, place the pencil tip on the starting point, and mark two other points along the bottom edge of the

triangle. Join these three points to make a line
at right angles to the edge of the page. Use a
straight edge to draw the line, and extend it
over seven and a half inches from the starting
point.

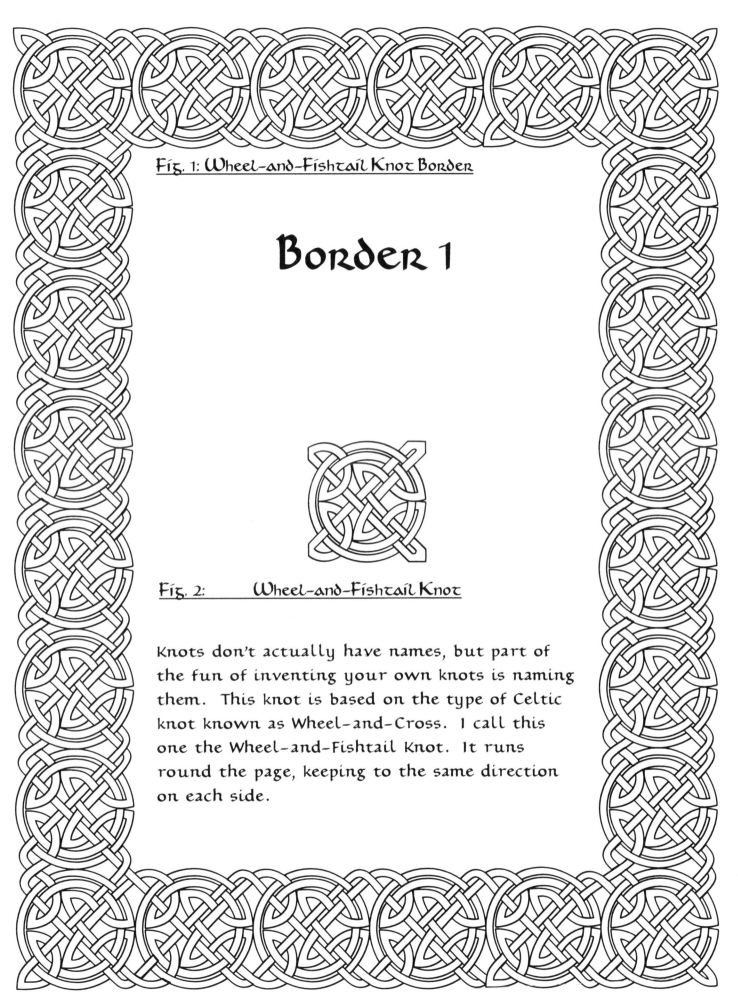

Fig. 1: Wheel-and-Fishtail Knot Border

Border 1

Fig. 2:   Wheel-and-Fishtail Knot

Knots don't actually have names, but part of
the fun of inventing your own knots is naming
them. This knot is based on the type of Celtic
knot known as Wheel-and-Cross. I call this
one the Wheel-and-Fishtail Knot. It runs
round the page, keeping to the same direction
on each side.

Fig. 3: The Versatile Grid

The grid is six squares across by eight squares down. Each square is $1\frac{1}{4}$" x $1\frac{1}{4}$". The knot fits one square unit.

The grid is $7\frac{1}{2}$" across x 10" down. This leaves a $\frac{1}{2}$" margin all around an $8\frac{1}{2}$"x 11" page.

Patterns based on this grid will fit on standard letter size paper.

This is a versatile grid, as we shall discover. It will take patterns based on units of one, two, three, four and six squares.

Fig. 4: Line Plan Layout for Four-Unit Strip

Fig. 5: Single Wheel-and-Fishtail Knot:

Step-by-step construction

a   Geometrical underlay.

b   Outer wheel connects to fish tail,
     inner wheel to diagonal cross.

c   Line plan for a single unit.

d   One knot, woven clockwise,
     or left-over-right.

e   The same knot, flipped vertically.

a   b

c   d   e

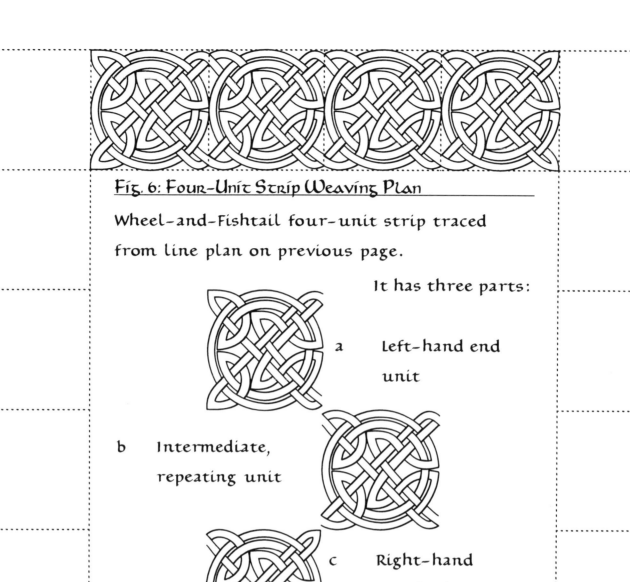

Fig. 6: Four-Unit Strip Weaving Plan

Wheel-and-Fishtail four-unit strip traced
from line plan on previous page.

It has three parts:

a   Left-hand end
       unit

b   Intermediate,
repeating unit

c   Right-hand
       terminal

Fig. 7: Three-Unit Border Strip Weaving Plan

Fig. 8: Six-Unit Border Strip Weaving Plan

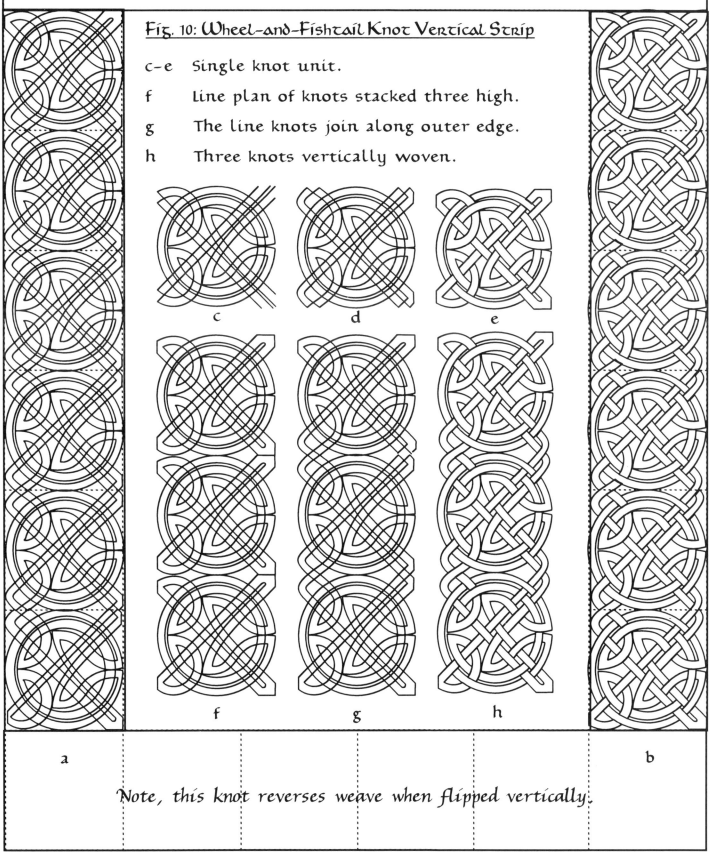

Fig. 9: Wheel-and-Fishtail Knot Vertical Strip

A six-square strip fits between the top and bottom edges of a 6x8 inch grid. On the left, a, is the line plan for the woven strip on the right, b.

Fig. 10: Wheel-and-Fishtail Knot Vertical Strip

c-e   Single knot unit.

f   Line plan of knots stacked three high.

g   The line knots join along outer edge.

h   Three knots vertically woven.

c   d   e

f   g   h

a   b

Note, this knot reverses weave when flipped vertically.

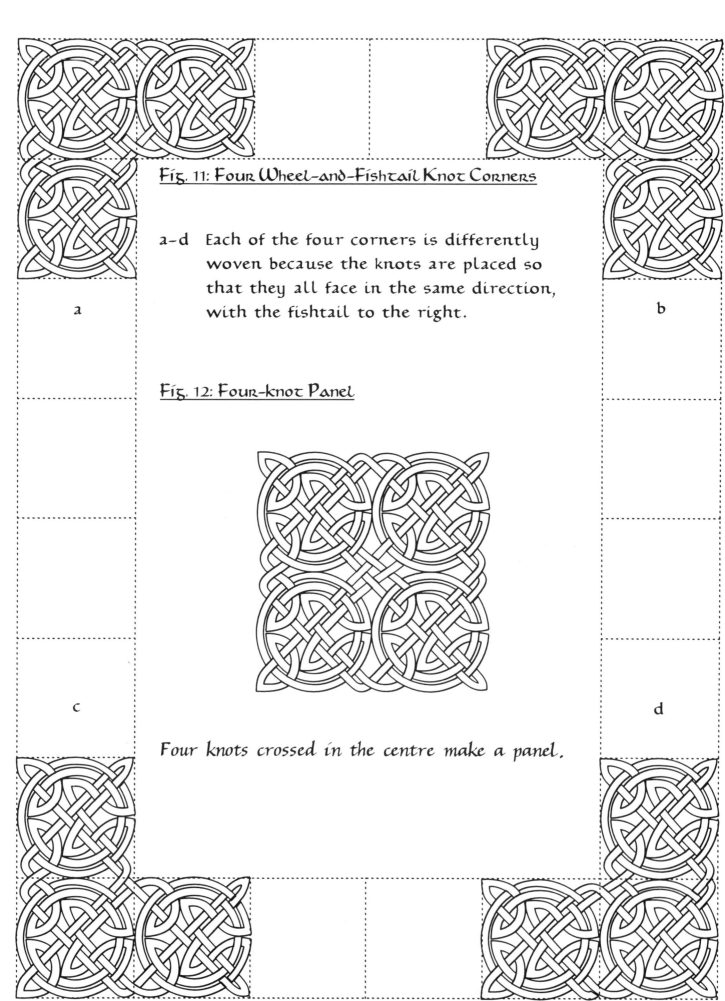

Fig. 11: Four Wheel-and-Fishtail Knot Corners

a–d Each of the four corners is differently
woven because the knots are placed so
that they all face in the same direction,
with the fishtail to the right.

Fig. 12: Four-knot Panel

a

b

c

d

Four knots crossed in the centre make a panel.

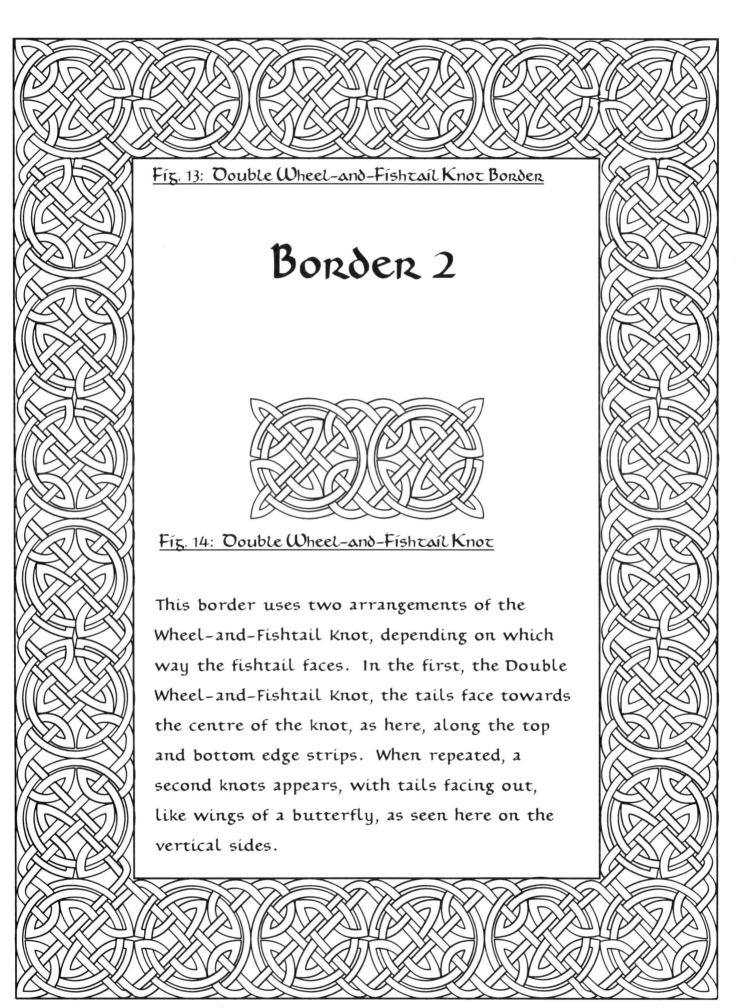

Fig. 13: Double Wheel-and-Fishtail Knot Border

Border 2

Fig. 14: Double Wheel-and-Fishtail Knot

This border uses two arrangements of the Wheel-and-Fishtail Knot, depending on which way the fishtail faces. In the first, the Double Wheel-and-Fishtail Knot, the tails face towards the centre of the knot, as here, along the top and bottom edge strips. When repeated, a second knots appears, with tails facing out, like wings of a butterfly, as seen here on the vertical sides.

Fig. 15: Double Wheel-and-Fishtail Border Layout

A six-by-eight square grid. The knot fits two square units.

a   Double Wheel-and-Fishtail Knot
b   Butterfly Knot

Fig. 16: Double Wheel-and-Fishtail Border Strips

a   Line plan, three squares wide.

b   Weaving plan for same.

c   Line plan, six squares wide.

d   Weaving plan for same.

a

b

c

d

Fig. 17: Double Wheel-and-Fishtail Border Strips

a   Line plan three squares wide, beginning with Butterfly.

b   Weaving plan for same.

c   Line plan, six squares, with Butterflies.

d   Weaving plan, six squares, with Butterflies.

a

b

c

d

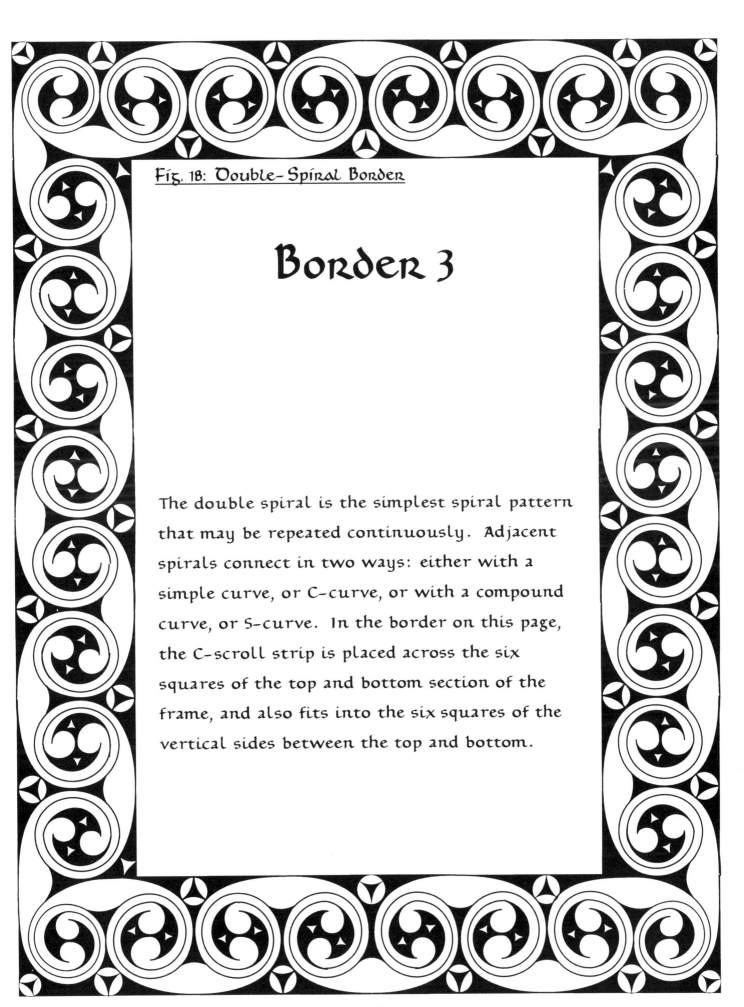

Fig. 18: Double-Spiral Border

Border 3

The double spiral is the simplest spiral pattern that may be repeated continuously. Adjacent spirals connect in two ways: either with a simple curve, or C-curve, or with a compound curve, or S-curve. In the border on this page, the C-scroll strip is placed across the six squares of the top and bottom section of the frame, and also fits into the six squares of the vertical sides between the top and bottom.

Fig. 19: Layout for Double-Spiral Border

The grid is six squares across by eight squares down. Eight spirals fit into six-unit strips.

a   C-curved double spiral.

b   Two C-curved double spirals make a C-scroll.

c   Interlocking C-scrolls.

In the C-curve arrangement, the double spirals are arranged in alternating directions.

Fig. 20: Double-Spiral Border Strips

a   Line plan for C–curved double spiral pair border strip, three squares wide.

b   Filled background plan for same.

c   Six–unit, open ended border strip.

d   Detail of two sides joined at right angles.

c

d

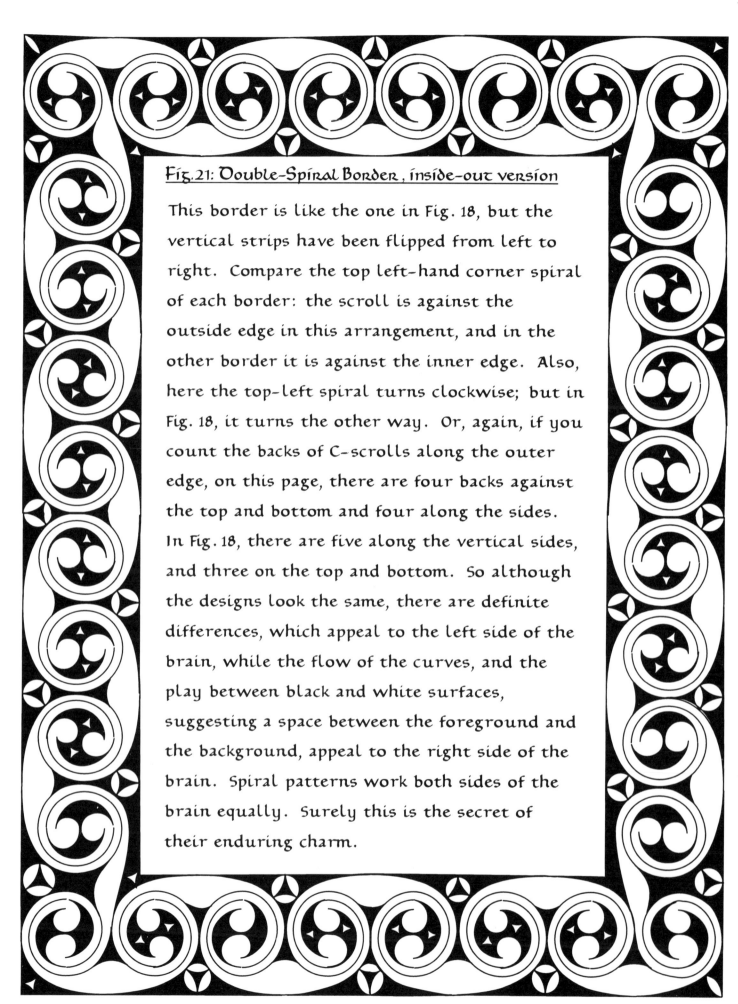

Fig. 21: Double-Spiral Border, inside-out version

This border is like the one in Fig. 18, but the vertical strips have been flipped from left to right. Compare the top left-hand corner spiral of each border: the scroll is against the outside edge in this arrangement, and in the other border it is against the inner edge. Also, here the top-left spiral turns clockwise; but in Fig. 18, it turns the other way. Or, again, if you count the backs of C-scrolls along the outer edge, on this page, there are four backs against the top and bottom and four along the sides. In Fig. 18, there are five along the vertical sides, and three on the top and bottom. So although the designs look the same, there are definite differences, which appeal to the left side of the brain, while the flow of the curves, and the play between black and white surfaces, suggesting a space between the foreground and the background, appeal to the right side of the brain. Spiral patterns work both sides of the brain equally. Surely this is the secret of their enduring charm.

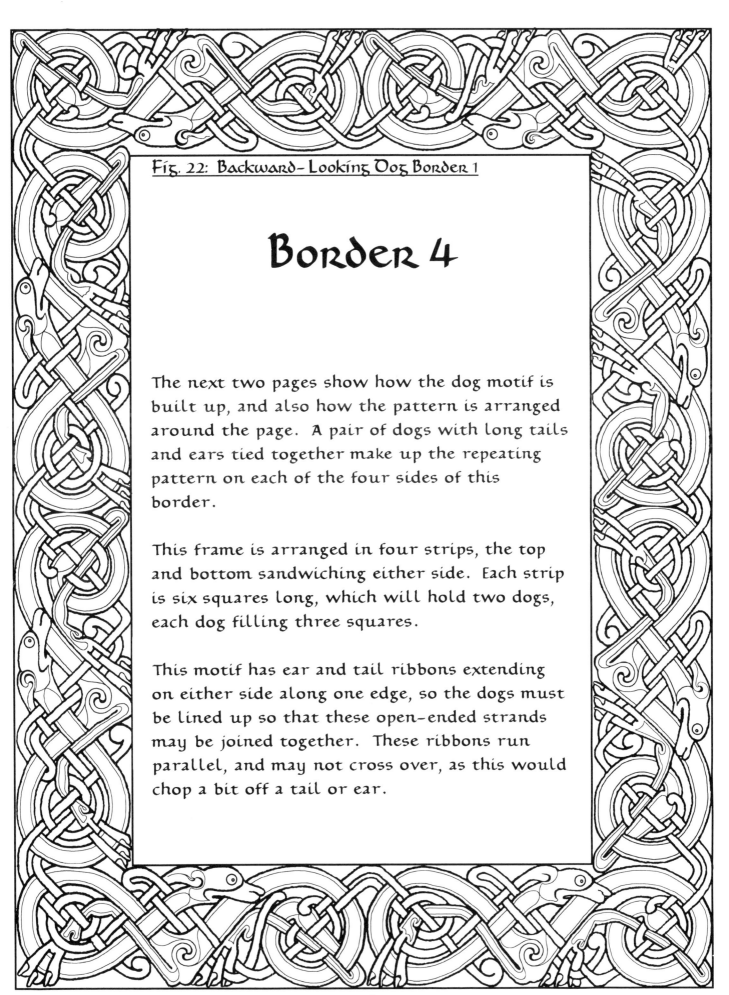

Fig. 22: Backward-Looking Dog Border 1

Border 4

The next two pages show how the dog motif is built up, and also how the pattern is arranged around the page. A pair of dogs with long tails and ears tied together make up the repeating pattern on each of the four sides of this border.

This frame is arranged in four strips, the top and bottom sandwiching either side. Each strip is six squares long, which will hold two dogs, each dog filling three squares.

This motif has ear and tail ribbons extending on either side along one edge, so the dogs must be lined up so that these open-ended strands may be joined together. These ribbons run parallel, and may not cross over, as this would chop a bit off a tail or ear.

Fig.23: Grid Layout and construction of Dog motif

a   Loop-necked dog's back coils in a spiral.

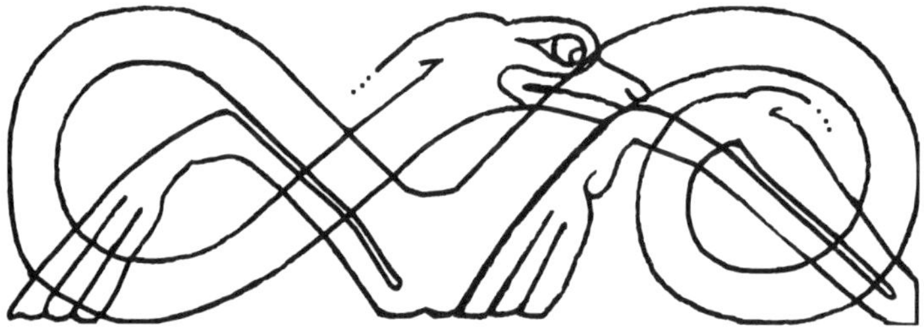

a

b   Pencilled lines for a long ear and a tail.

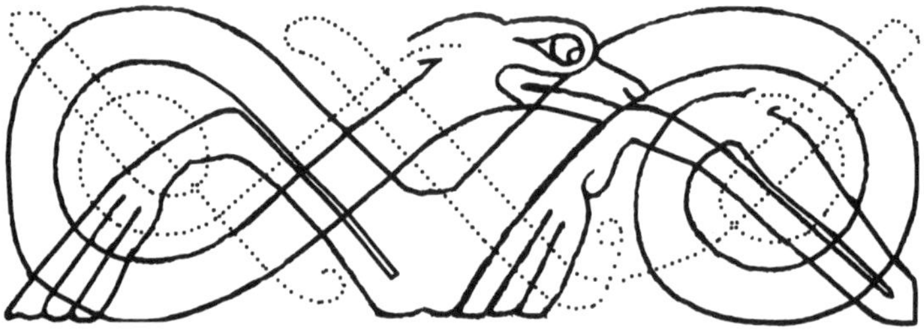

b

c   Line Plan, now ready to weave.

c

d   Stencil plan traced from previous step.

d

e   line plan: ear and tail are left open ended.

e

f   Weave first strand over-under, and so on.

f

g   Check weave is correct, then ink up.

g

h   Add hairline contour as finishing touch.

h

Fig. 24: Two Border Strips joined as Corner Bracket

The two dogs along the top are the same as those along the side, only turned 90°. The corner is mitred by joining the open-ended strands of the animals' tails. These two strands must not be crossed, or this would spoil the design.

a   (Top edge) Two dogs connected in a strip.

b   (Left side) The same unit, turned 90°, with open-ended strands lined up ready to be joined.

c   (Below, right) Both units make one half of a full-page border and a corner bracket design.

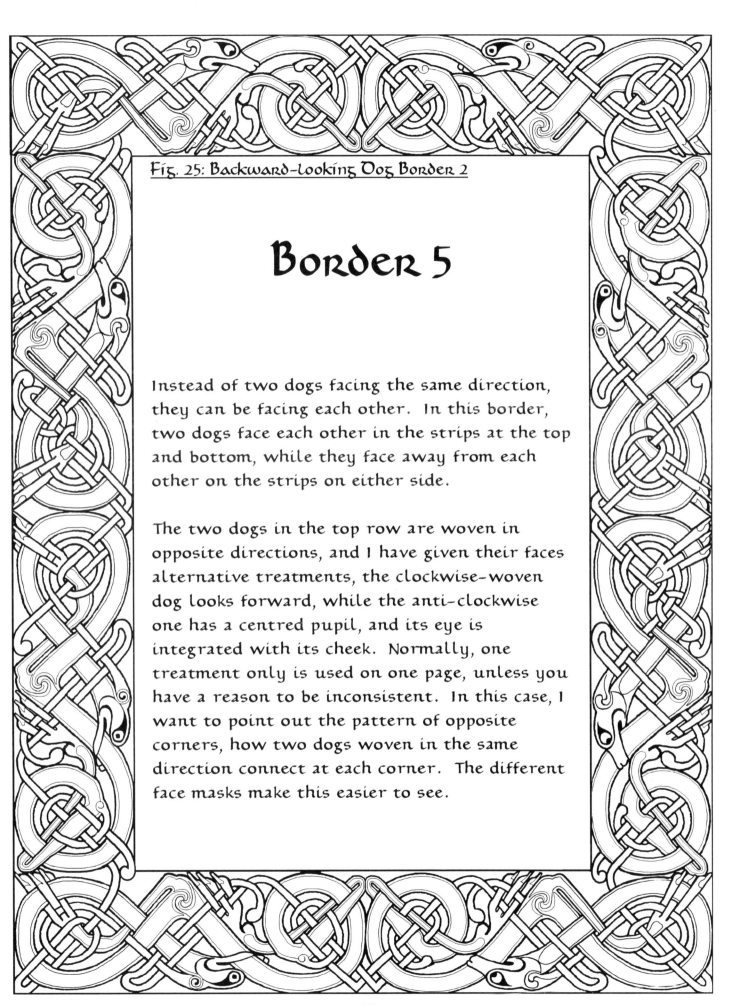

Fig. 25: Backward-looking Dog Border 2

Border 5

Instead of two dogs facing the same direction, they can be facing each other. In this border, two dogs face each other in the strips at the top and bottom, while they face away from each other on the strips on either side.

The two dogs in the top row are woven in opposite directions, and I have given their faces alternative treatments, the clockwise-woven dog looks forward, while the anti-clockwise one has a centred pupil, and its eye is integrated with its cheek. Normally, one treatment only is used on one page, unless you have a reason to be inconsistent. In this case, I want to point out the pattern of opposite corners, how two dogs woven in the same direction connect at each corner. The different face masks make this easier to see.

Fig. 26: Flipped Stencil Layout Plan

a   Stencilled dog facing right

a

b   Stencilled dog facing left

b

This frame is arranged as before, each pair fits six squares, mitred with the top and bottom sandwiching either side. To make a double unit, trace the stencil design from the line plan, Border 4, Fig. 23e.

Flip the tracing over, Fig. 26b, and place it pencilled side down on a scrap of paper, such as a blank sheet on a pad of newsprint paper. Now trace through from the other side to produce a mirror image on each side of the tracing paper, so that by flipping the tracing over you can reverse the direction of the image as you need.

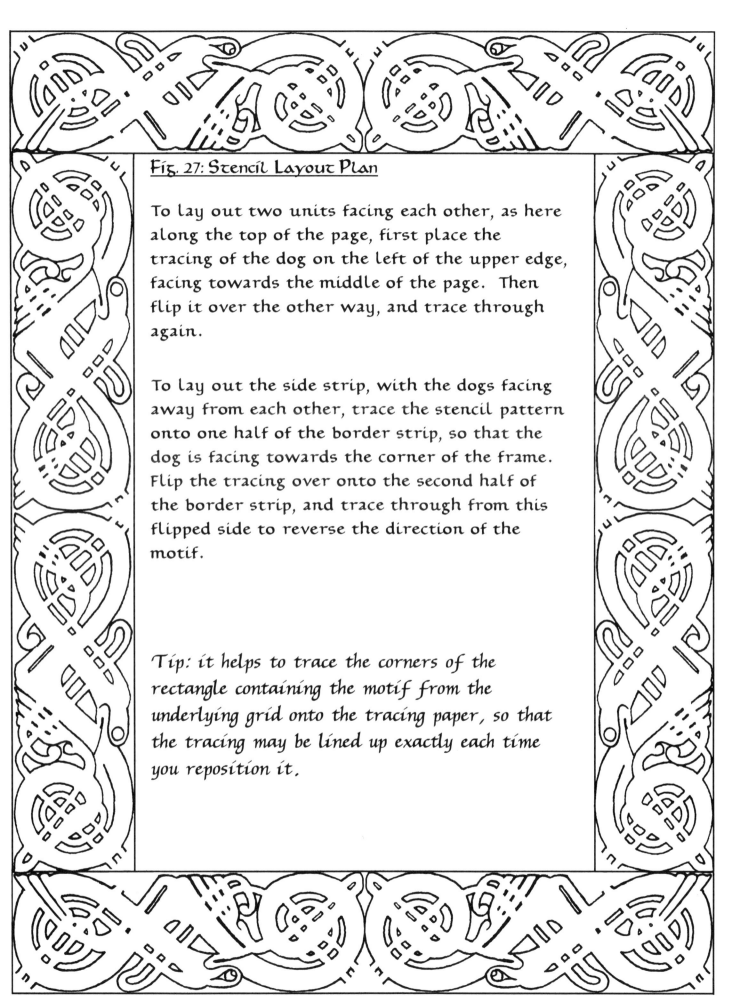

Fig. 27: Stencil Layout Plan

To lay out two units facing each other, as here along the top of the page, first place the tracing of the dog on the left of the upper edge, facing towards the middle of the page. Then flip it over the other way, and trace through again.

To lay out the side strip, with the dogs facing away from each other, trace the stencil pattern onto one half of the border strip, so that the dog is facing towards the corner of the frame. Flip the tracing over onto the second half of the border strip, and trace through from this flipped side to reverse the direction of the motif.

Tip: it helps to trace the corners of the rectangle containing the motif from the underlying grid onto the tracing paper, so that the tracing may be lined up exactly each time you reposition it.

Fig. 28: Linking Two Stencil Units in a Corner

Tip: do not join the ear and tail here, as this will orphan a strand.

Fig. 29: Weaving Plan

a

b

a   Weaving starts in the upper left-hand corner, and passes over the dog's neck.

b   Weaving starts in upper left-hand corner, and passes over the dog's spine.

Whichever way the motif faces, the ear and tail ribbons still extend to either side along the same edge. Now, the opposite-facing stencil tracings must be woven so that the open strands may join together. Each pair of opposite-facing dogs needs to be woven in reverse, as the weaving must keep to one direction throughout.

Fig: 30: Backward-Looking Dog Border Strip, six-squares, two variations

a, b, c   Border strip of two dogs looking towards each other.

d, e, f   Border strip of two dogs looking away from each other.

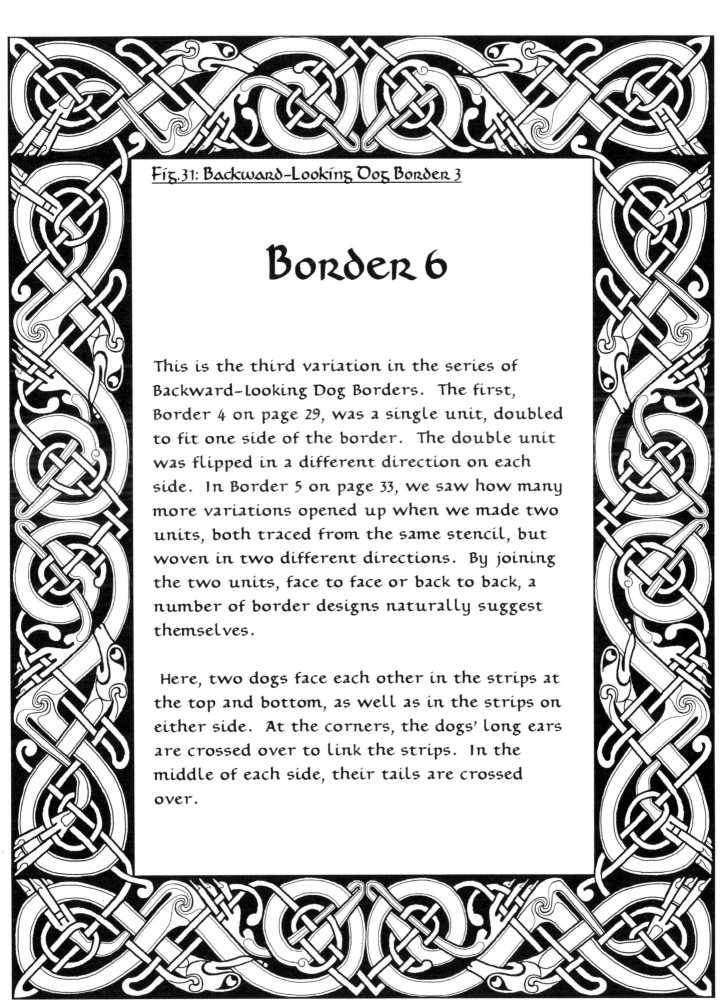

Border 6

This is the third variation in the series of Backward-Looking Dog Borders. The first, Border 4 on page 29, was a single unit, doubled to fit one side of the border. The double unit was flipped in a different direction on each side. In Border 5 on page 33, we saw how many more variations opened up when we made two units, both traced from the same stencil, but woven in two different directions. By joining the two units, face to face or back to back, a number of border designs naturally suggest themselves.

Here, two dogs face each other in the strips at the top and bottom, as well as in the strips on either side. At the corners, the dogs' long ears are crossed over to link the strips. In the middle of each side, their tails are crossed over.

Fig. 32: Backward-Looking Dog Border 3, Layout

The layout here is the same as before, six squares across the top and bottom and six in between.

The unit is a pair of dogs, each traced off the same underlying line pattern, but woven in opposite directions. Or, traced off the same stencil, each half of the pair a mirror image, which is then woven in the same direction throughout. There are two ways to read the design, and both are equally valid. The same pattern may be read in one way, or the other, like an optical illusion. It is a brain teaser.

However, when the two opposite-facing dogs are woven together, another strange thing happens. If you trace the woven pair, you can flip the tracing over, and you have the same pair of dogs as before, only now they have kindly re-woven themselves in the opposite direction. Very handy for laying out two sides at a time.

The strip at the top of this page is woven in one direction, beginning at the top left-hand corner and then over to the right, that is, right-turning or clockwise. The strip below is the same design flipped horizontally, so that the weaving is reversed, crossing anti-clockwise.

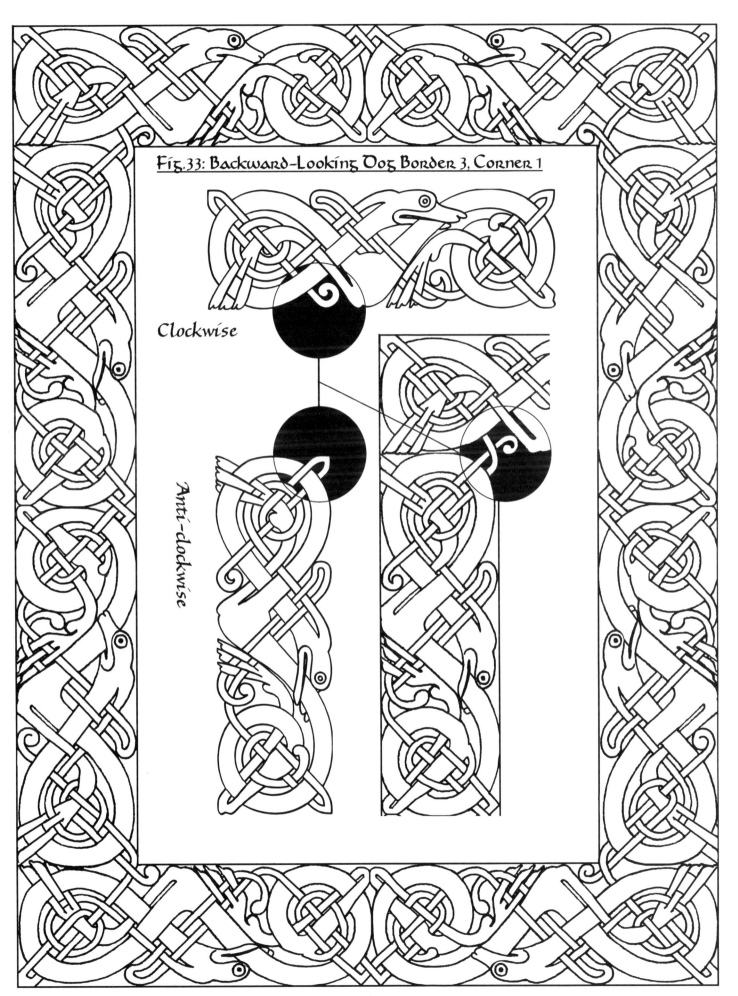

Fig. 33: Backward-Looking Dog Border 3, Corner 1

Clockwise

Anti-clockwise

41

Fig.34: Backward-Looking Dog Border 3, Corner 2

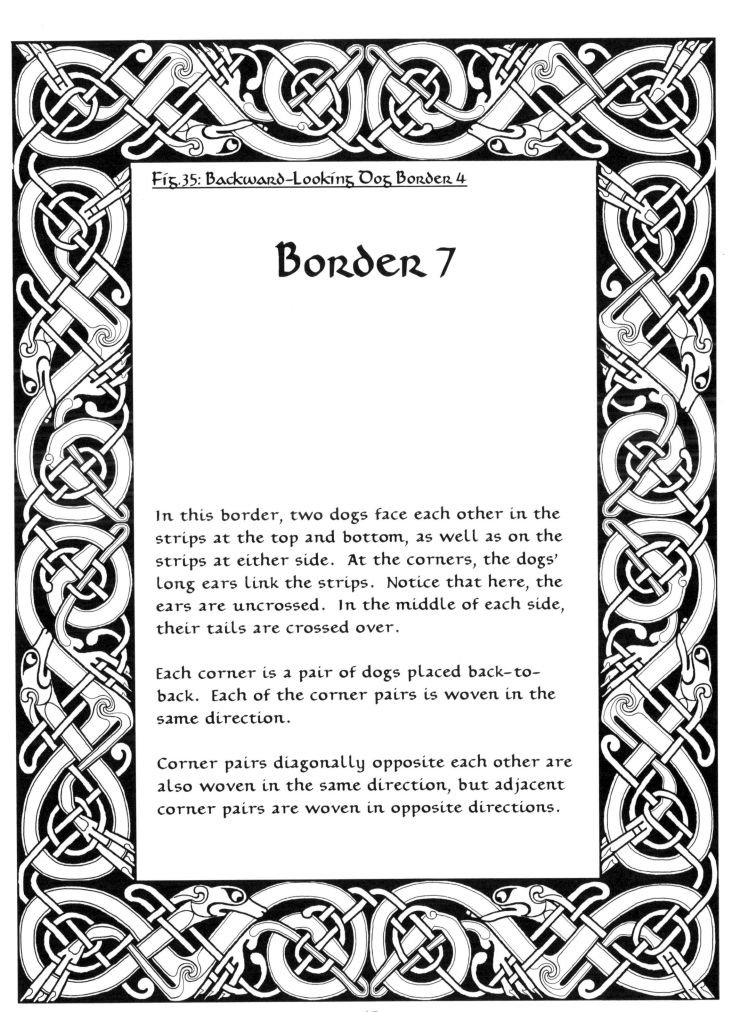

Border 7

In this border, two dogs face each other in the strips at the top and bottom, as well as on the strips at either side. At the corners, the dogs' long ears link the strips. Notice that here, the ears are uncrossed. In the middle of each side, their tails are crossed over.

Each corner is a pair of dogs placed back-to-back. Each of the corner pairs is woven in the same direction.

Corner pairs diagonally opposite each other are also woven in the same direction, but adjacent corner pairs are woven in opposite directions.

Fig. 36: Backward-Looking Dog Border 4, Corner 1

Fig.37: Backward-Looking Dog Border 4, Corner 2

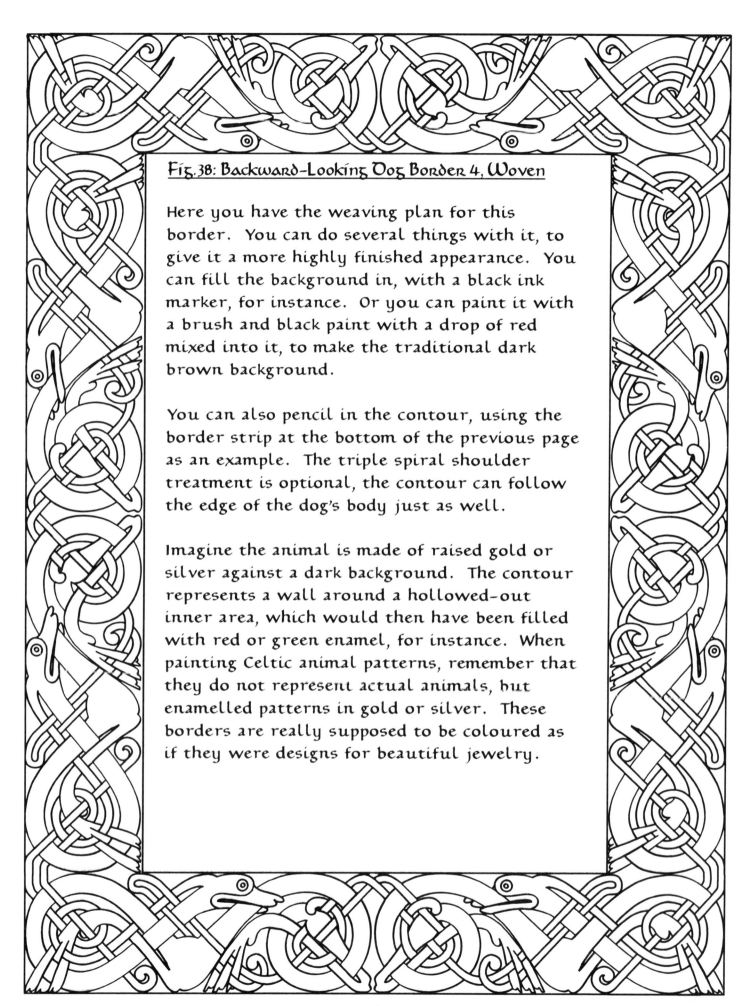

Fig. 38: Backward-Looking Dog Border 4, Woven

Here you have the weaving plan for this border. You can do several things with it, to give it a more highly finished appearance. You can fill the background in, with a black ink marker, for instance. Or you can paint it with a brush and black paint with a drop of red mixed into it, to make the traditional dark brown background.

You can also pencil in the contour, using the border strip at the bottom of the previous page as an example. The triple spiral shoulder treatment is optional, the contour can follow the edge of the dog's body just as well.

Imagine the animal is made of raised gold or silver against a dark background. The contour represents a wall around a hollowed-out inner area, which would then have been filled with red or green enamel, for instance. When painting Celtic animal patterns, remember that they do not represent actual animals, but enamelled patterns in gold or silver. These borders are really supposed to be coloured as if they were designs for beautiful jewelry.

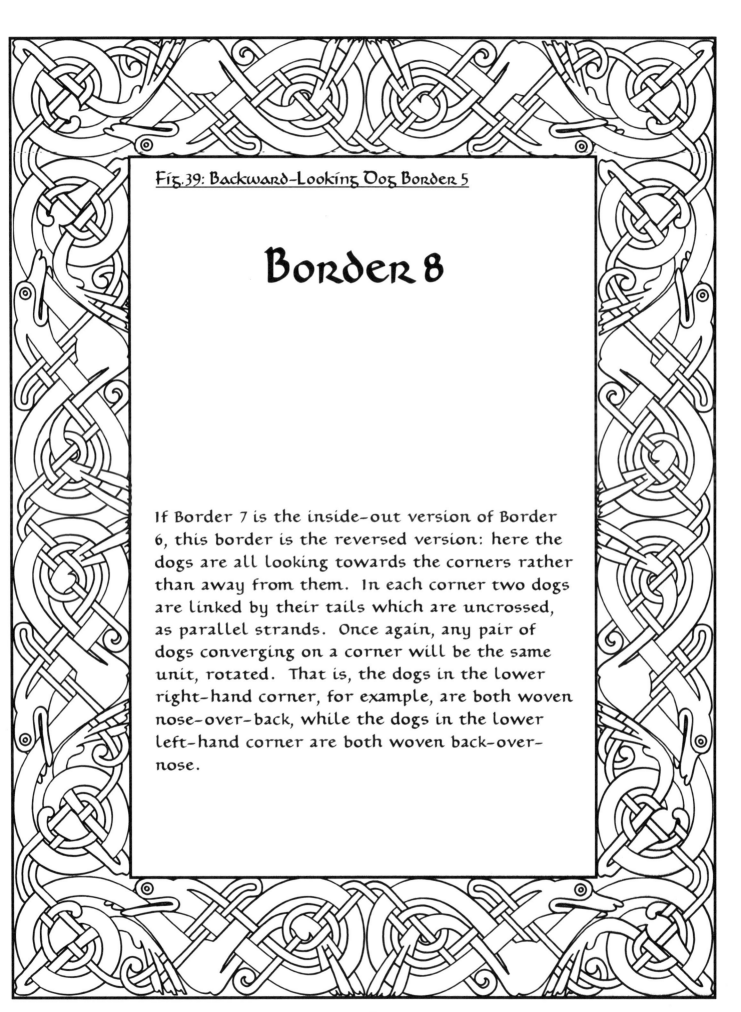

Border 8

If Border 7 is the inside-out version of Border 6, this border is the reversed version: here the dogs are all looking towards the corners rather than away from them. In each corner two dogs are linked by their tails which are uncrossed, as parallel strands. Once again, any pair of dogs converging on a corner will be the same unit, rotated. That is, the dogs in the lower right-hand corner, for example, are both woven nose-over-back, while the dogs in the lower left-hand corner are both woven back-over-nose.

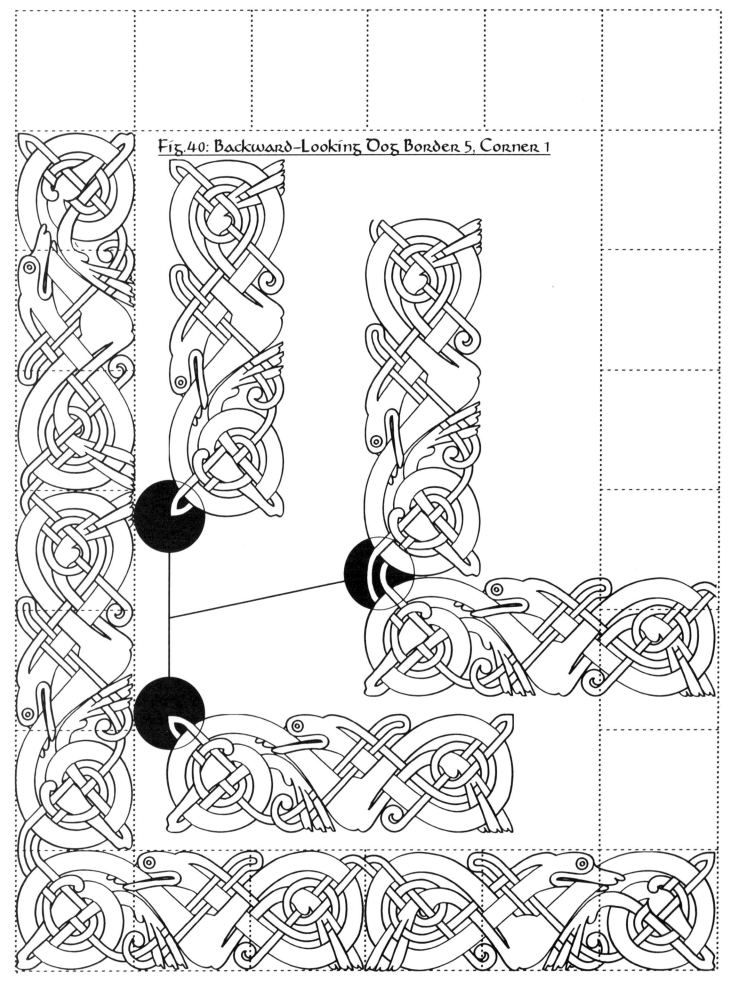

Fig.40: Backward-Looking Dog Border 5, Corner 1

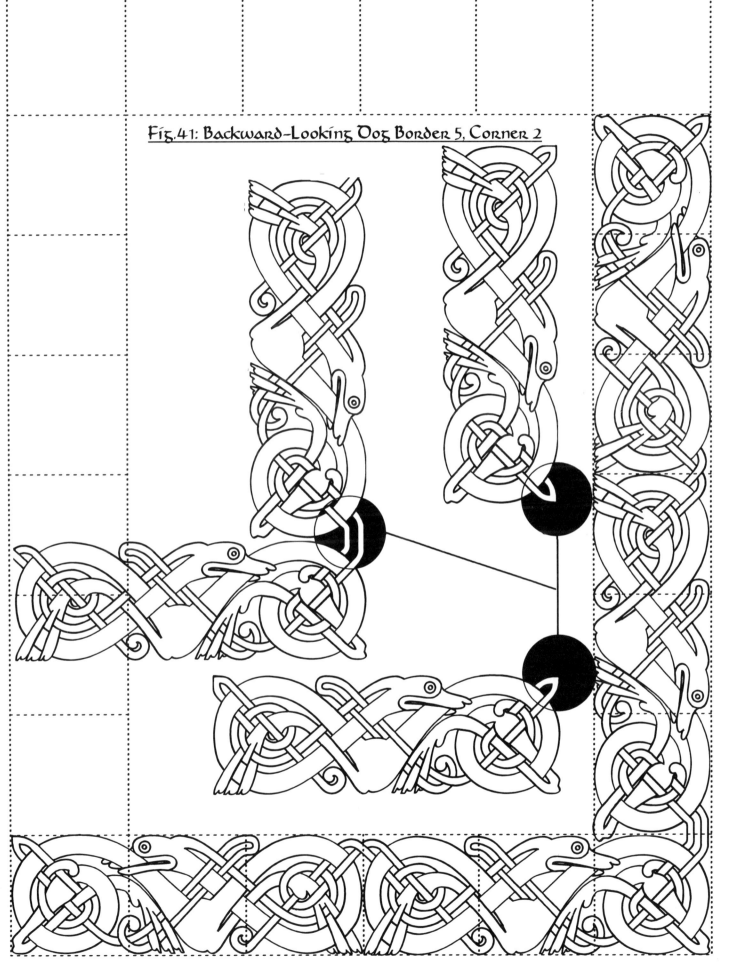

Fig.41: Backward-Looking Dog Border 5, Corner 2

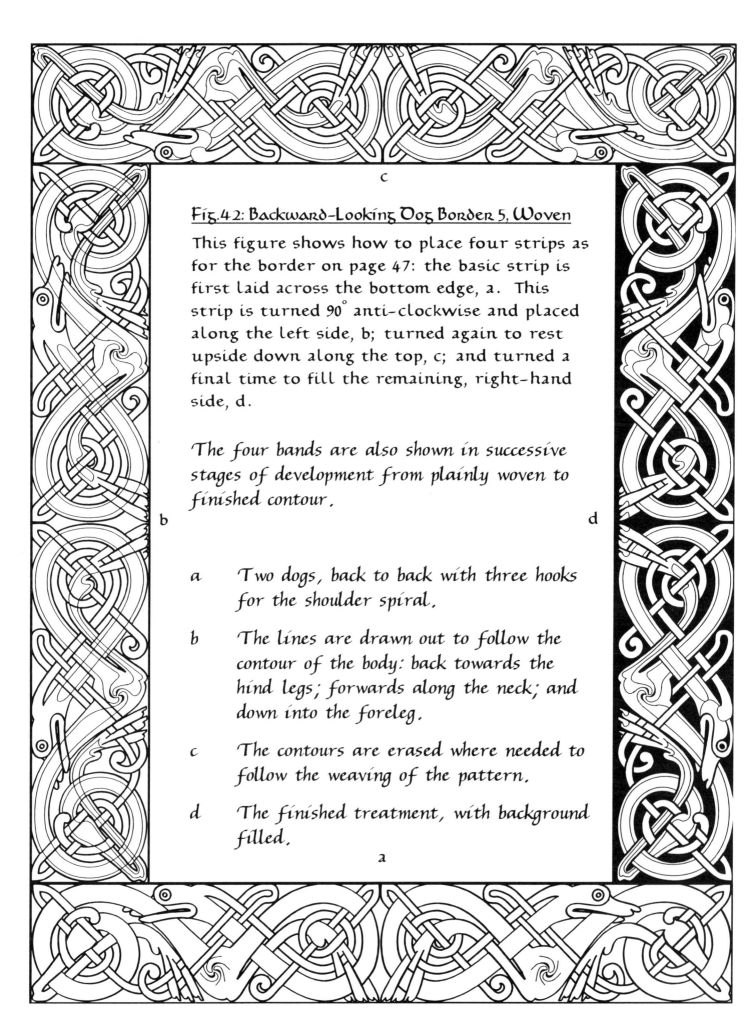

c

Fig. 42: Backward-Looking Dog Border 5, Woven

This figure shows how to place four strips as for the border on page 47: the basic strip is first laid across the bottom edge, a. This strip is turned 90° anti-clockwise and placed along the left side, b; turned again to rest upside down along the top, c; and turned a final time to fill the remaining, right-hand side, d.

The four bands are also shown in successive stages of development from plainly woven to finished contour.

b

d

a   Two dogs, back to back with three hooks for the shoulder spiral.

b   The lines are drawn out to follow the contour of the body: back towards the hind legs; forwards along the neck; and down into the foreleg.

c   The contours are erased where needed to follow the weaving of the pattern.

d   The finished treatment, with background filled.

a

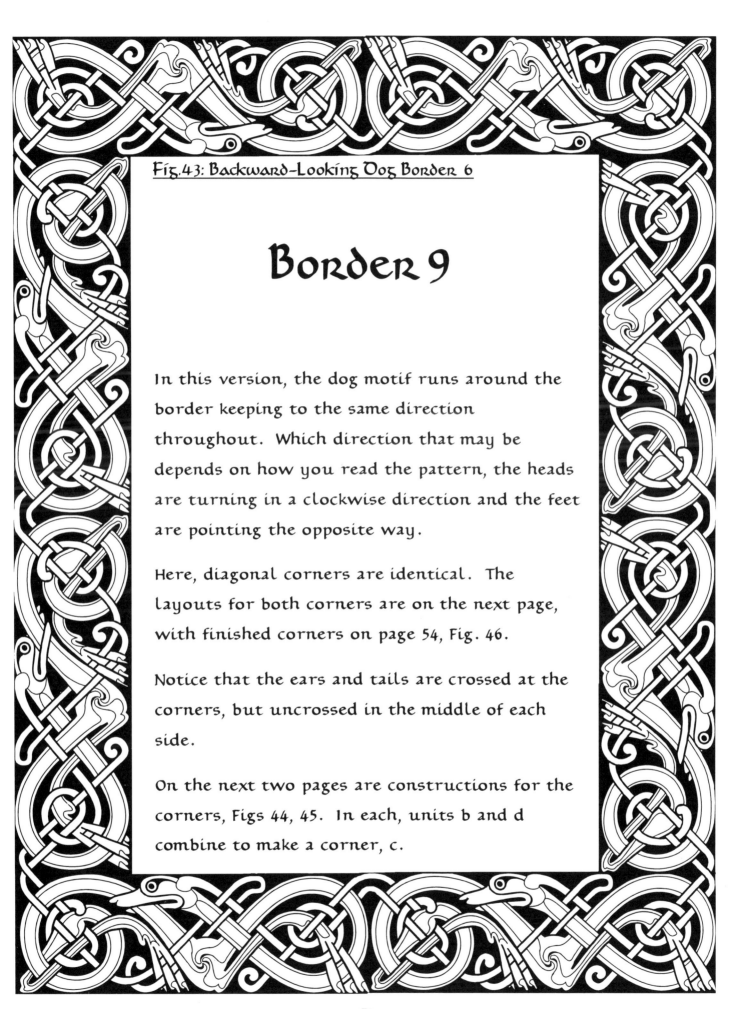

Border 9

In this version, the dog motif runs around the border keeping to the same direction throughout. Which direction that may be depends on how you read the pattern, the heads are turning in a clockwise direction and the feet are pointing the opposite way.

Here, diagonal corners are identical. The layouts for both corners are on the next page, with finished corners on page 54, Fig. 46.

Notice that the ears and tails are crossed at the corners, but uncrossed in the middle of each side.

On the next two pages are constructions for the corners, Figs 44, 45. In each, units b and d combine to make a corner, c.

Fig.44: Backward-Looking Dog Border 6, Layout 1

a

b

c

d

52

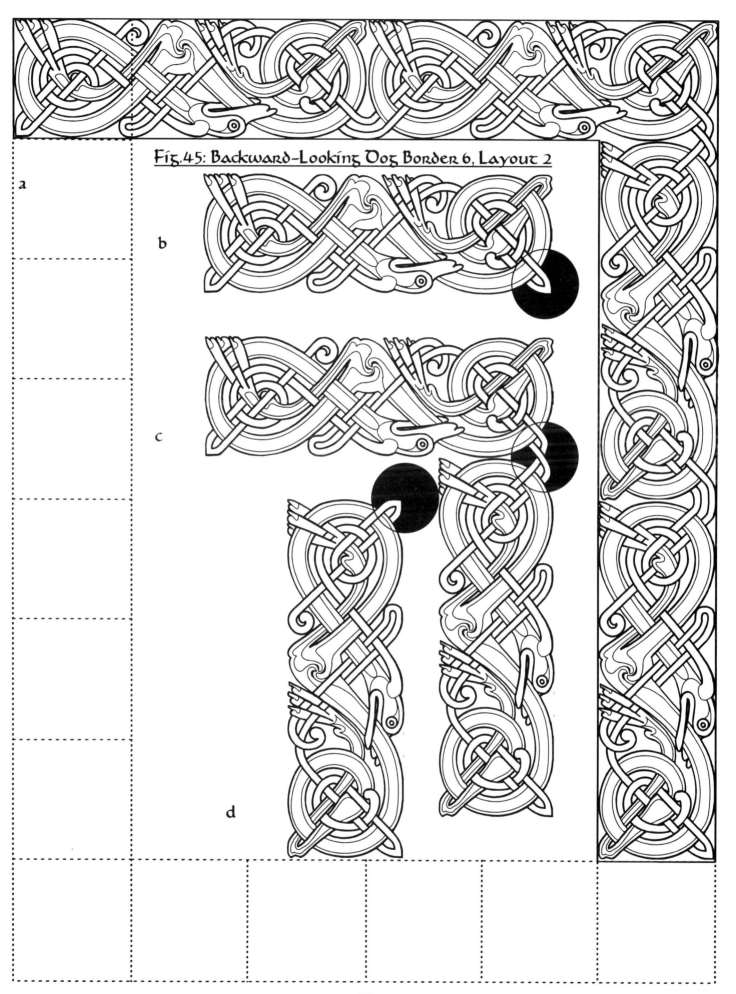

Fig.45: Backward-Looking Dog Border 6, Layout 2

a

b

c

d

Fig.46: Backward-Looking Dog Border 6, Corners

a

b

c

d

The dogs are woven clockwise, a, and anti-clockwise, b. In the smaller bracket, c, the two units are linked by crossing ear and tail. Here, unit b is rotated 180°, while unit a is rotated 90°, and then flipped. In the larger bracket, d, the corner is expanded by one unit on each side. Unit b is repeated on the bottom edge, the units bridged by two parallel strands consisting of ear and tail, uncrossed. Unit a is repeated on the vertical side, likewise bridged by parallel strands.

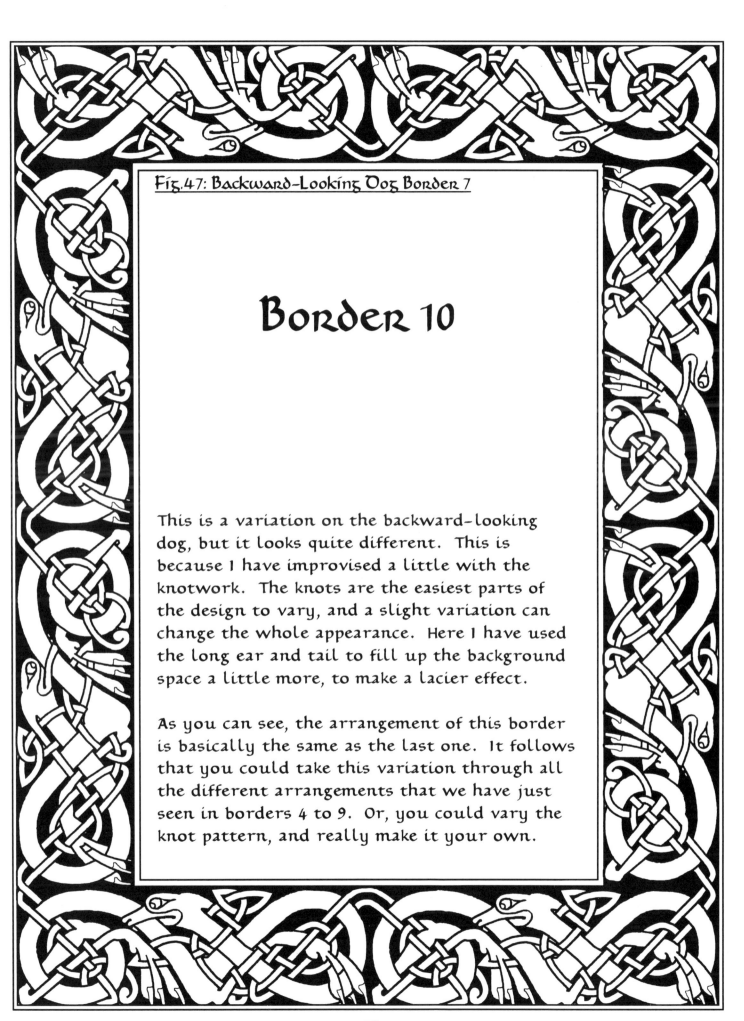

Border 10

This is a variation on the backward-looking dog, but it looks quite different. This is because I have improvised a little with the knotwork. The knots are the easiest parts of the design to vary, and a slight variation can change the whole appearance. Here I have used the long ear and tail to fill up the background space a little more, to make a lacier effect.

As you can see, the arrangement of this border is basically the same as the last one. It follows that you could take this variation through all the different arrangements that we have just seen in borders 4 to 9. Or, you could vary the knot pattern, and really make it your own.

Fig.48: Backward-Looking Dog Border 7, Layout 1

a

The dotted line represents the pencilled plan for the ear and tail knots.

b

The line plan. Notice that the path of each knot ends outside the area of the weaving. If it stops inside, it may cause a dropped stitch, over-over or under-under.

c

The stencil plan, derived from the line plan.

Fig.49: Backward-Looking Dog Border 7, Layout 2

a

This dog is facing left, and woven in an anti-clockwise direction.

b

This one is facing right, but woven in the same direction. Compare with Fig. 49c, which is the same as Fig. 49a flipped.

c

Facing to the right, woven clockwise.

Fig. 50: Backward-Looking Dog Border 7, Woven

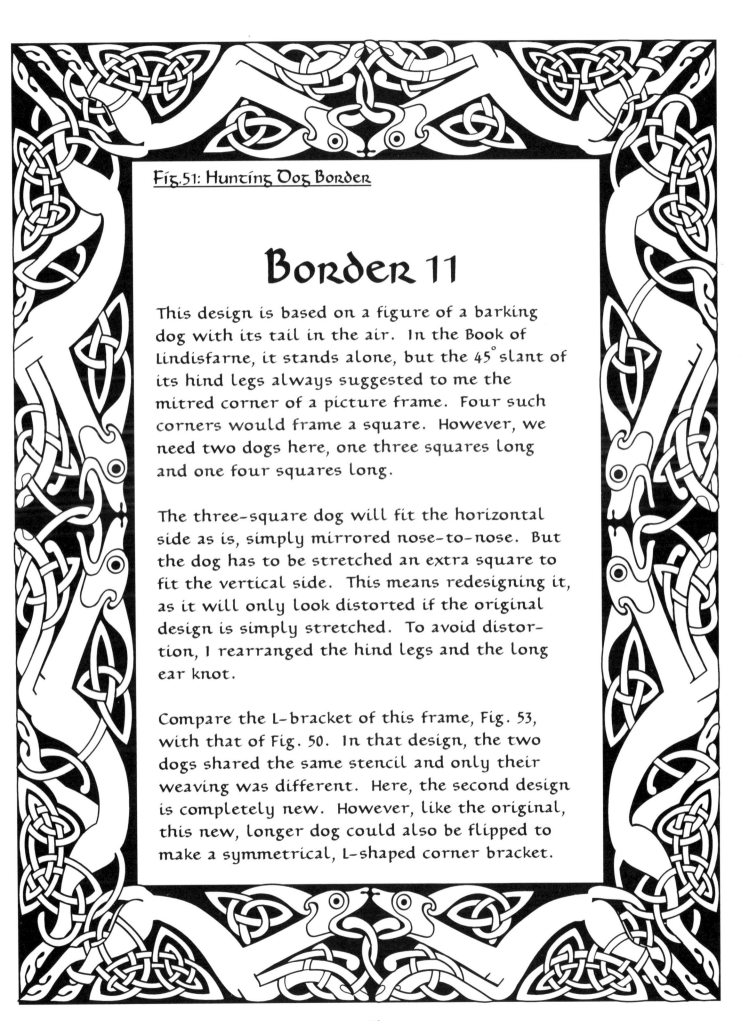

Fig. 51: Hunting Dog Border

Border 11

This design is based on a figure of a barking dog with its tail in the air. In the Book of Lindisfarne, it stands alone, but the $45°$ slant of its hind legs always suggested to me the mitred corner of a picture frame. Four such corners would frame a square. However, we need two dogs here, one three squares long and one four squares long.

The three-square dog will fit the horizontal side as is, simply mirrored nose-to-nose. But the dog has to be stretched an extra square to fit the vertical side. This means redesigning it, as it will only look distorted if the original design is simply stretched. To avoid distortion, I rearranged the hind legs and the long ear knot.

Compare the L-bracket of this frame, Fig. 53, with that of Fig. 50. In that design, the two dogs shared the same stencil and only their weaving was different. Here, the second design is completely new. However, like the original, this new, longer dog could also be flipped to make a symmetrical, L-shaped corner bracket.

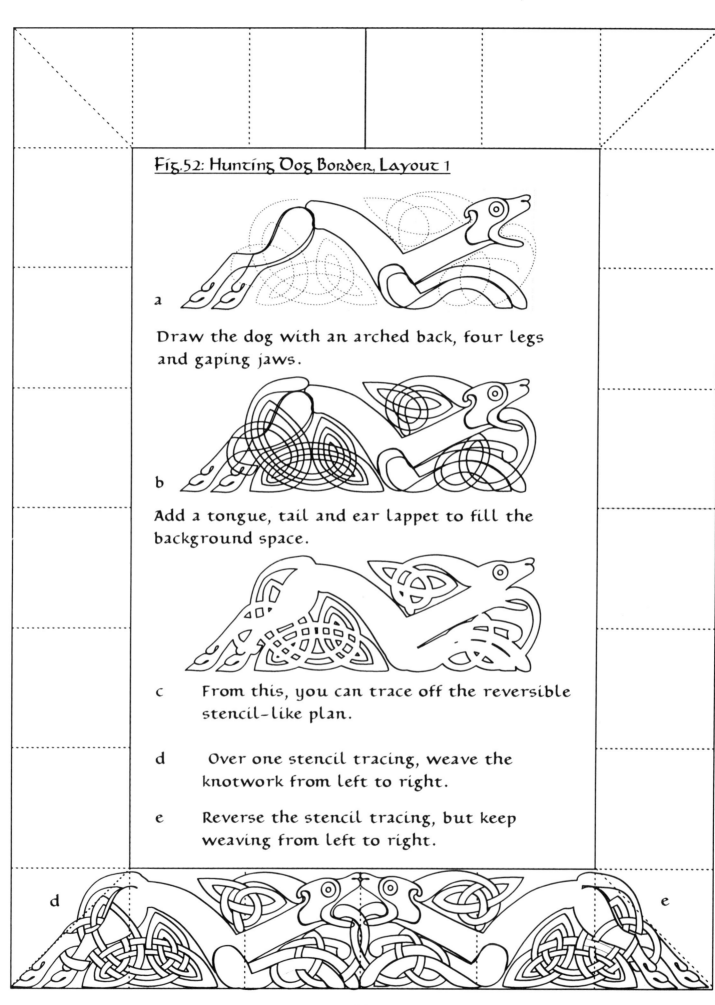

Fig.52: Hunting Dog Border, Layout 1

a

Draw the dog with an arched back, four legs and gaping jaws.

b

Add a tongue, tail and ear lappet to fill the background space.

c   From this, you can trace off the reversible stencil-like plan.

d   Over one stencil tracing, weave the knotwork from left to right.

e   Reverse the stencil tracing, but keep weaving from left to right.

d   e

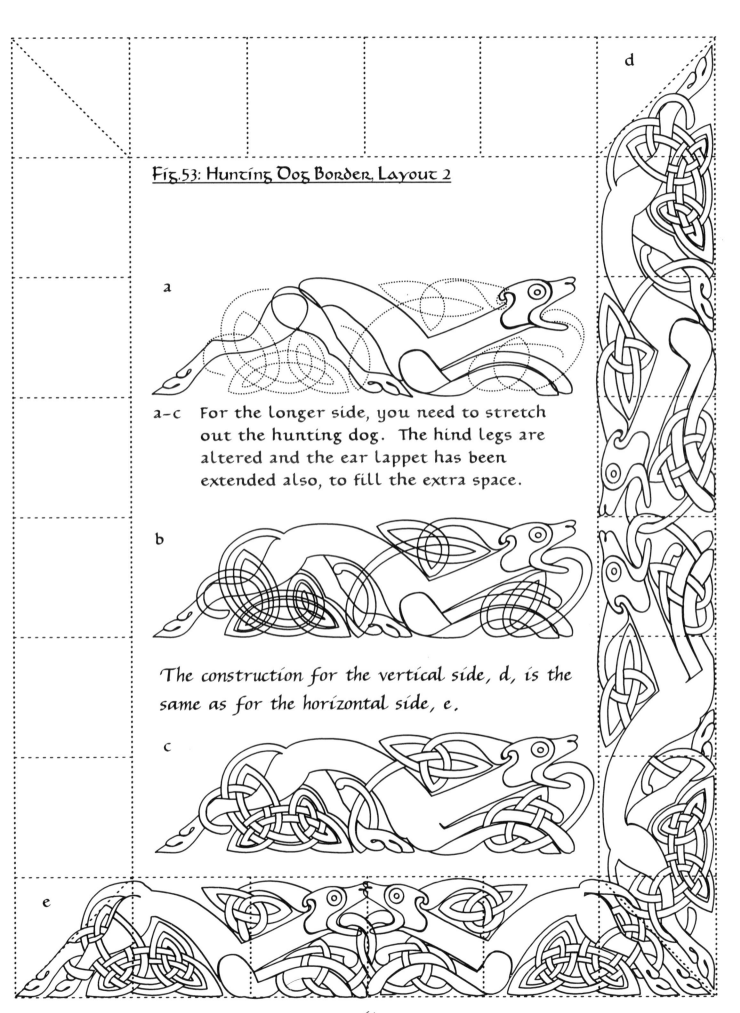

Fig. 53: Hunting Dog Border, Layout 2

a

a–c For the longer side, you need to stretch out the hunting dog. The hind legs are altered and the ear lappet has been extended also, to fill the extra space.

b

The construction for the vertical side, d, is the same as for the horizontal side, e.

c

d

e

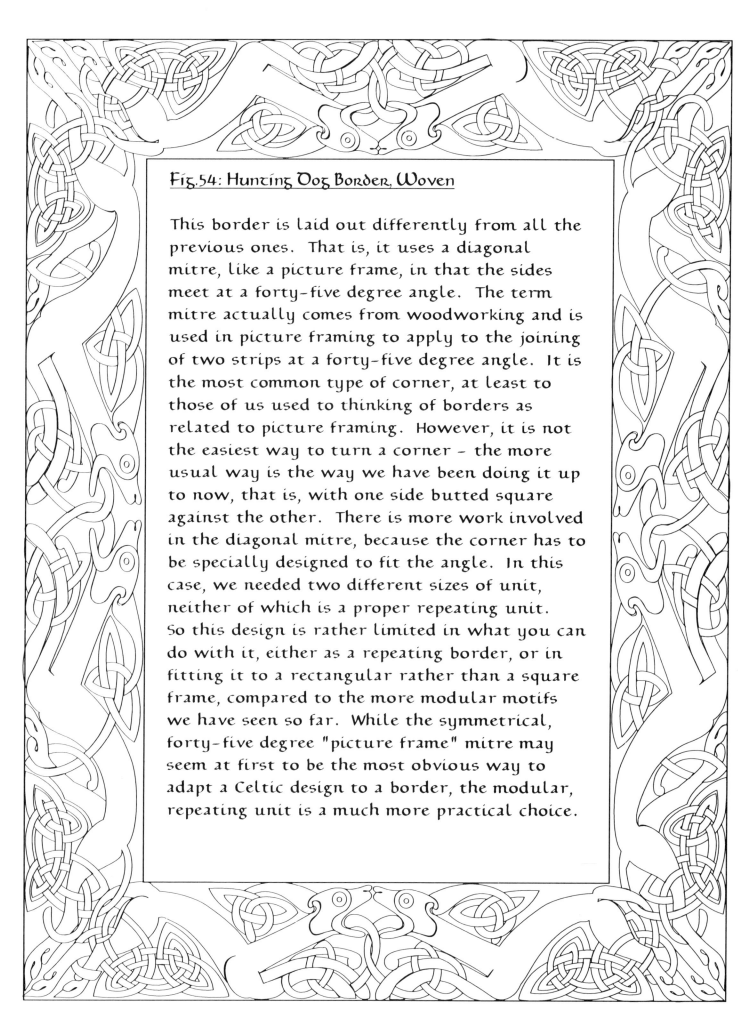

Fig.54: Hunting Dog Border, Woven

This border is laid out differently from all the previous ones. That is, it uses a diagonal mitre, like a picture frame, in that the sides meet at a forty-five degree angle. The term mitre actually comes from woodworking and is used in picture framing to apply to the joining of two strips at a forty-five degree angle. It is the most common type of corner, at least to those of us used to thinking of borders as related to picture framing. However, it is not the easiest way to turn a corner – the more usual way is the way we have been doing it up to now, that is, with one side butted square against the other. There is more work involved in the diagonal mitre, because the corner has to be specially designed to fit the angle. In this case, we needed two different sizes of unit, neither of which is a proper repeating unit. So this design is rather limited in what you can do with it, either as a repeating border, or in fitting it to a rectangular rather than a square frame, compared to the more modular motifs we have seen so far. While the symmetrical, forty-five degree "picture frame" mitre may seem at first to be the most obvious way to adapt a Celtic design to a border, the modular, repeating unit is a much more practical choice.

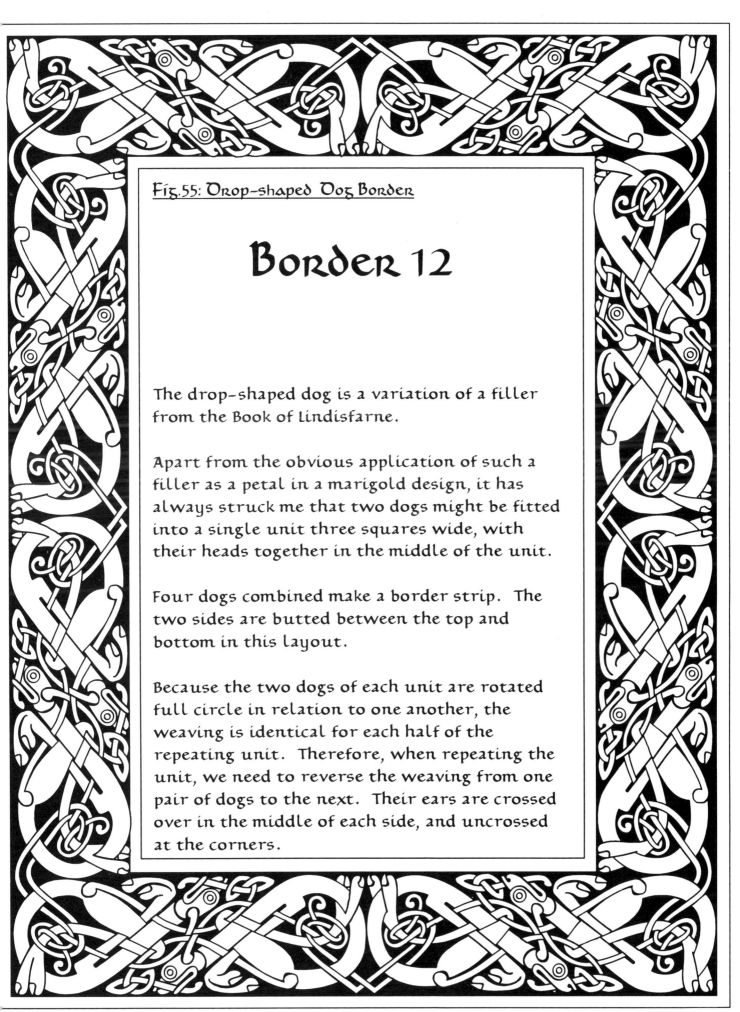

Border 12

The drop-shaped dog is a variation of a filler from the Book of Lindisfarne.

Apart from the obvious application of such a filler as a petal in a marigold design, it has always struck me that two dogs might be fitted into a single unit three squares wide, with their heads together in the middle of the unit.

Four dogs combined make a border strip. The two sides are butted between the top and bottom in this layout.

Because the two dogs of each unit are rotated full circle in relation to one another, the weaving is identical for each half of the repeating unit. Therefore, when repeating the unit, we need to reverse the weaving from one pair of dogs to the next. Their ears are crossed over in the middle of each side, and uncrossed at the corners.

Fig.56: Drop-shaped Dog Border, Layout 1

a   The basic drop-shaped dog.

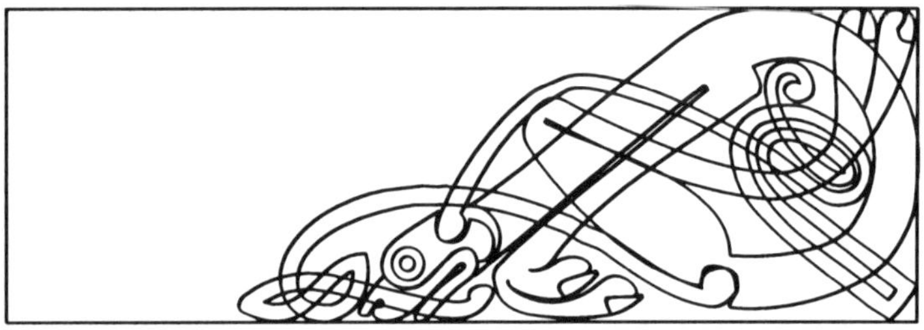

b   Ears and tail added, line plan for one dog.

c   Line plan for two dogs.

d   Repeating unit, clockwise weaving plan.

e

64

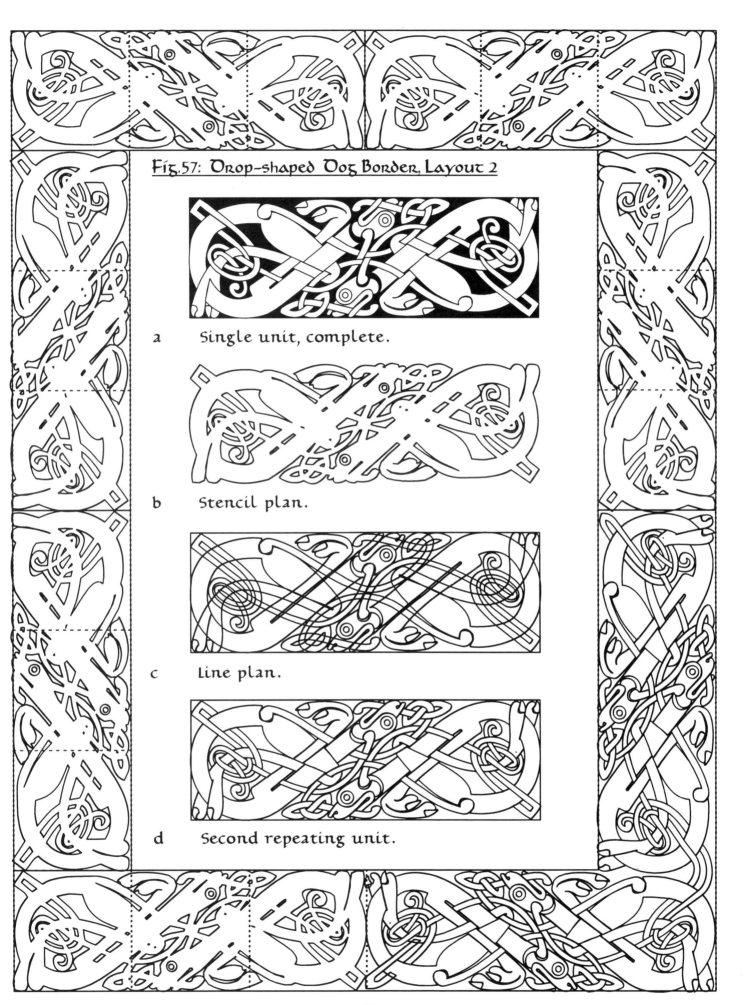

Fig.57: Drop-shaped Dog Border, Layout 2

a   Single unit, complete.

b   Stencil plan.

c   Line plan.

d   Second repeating unit.

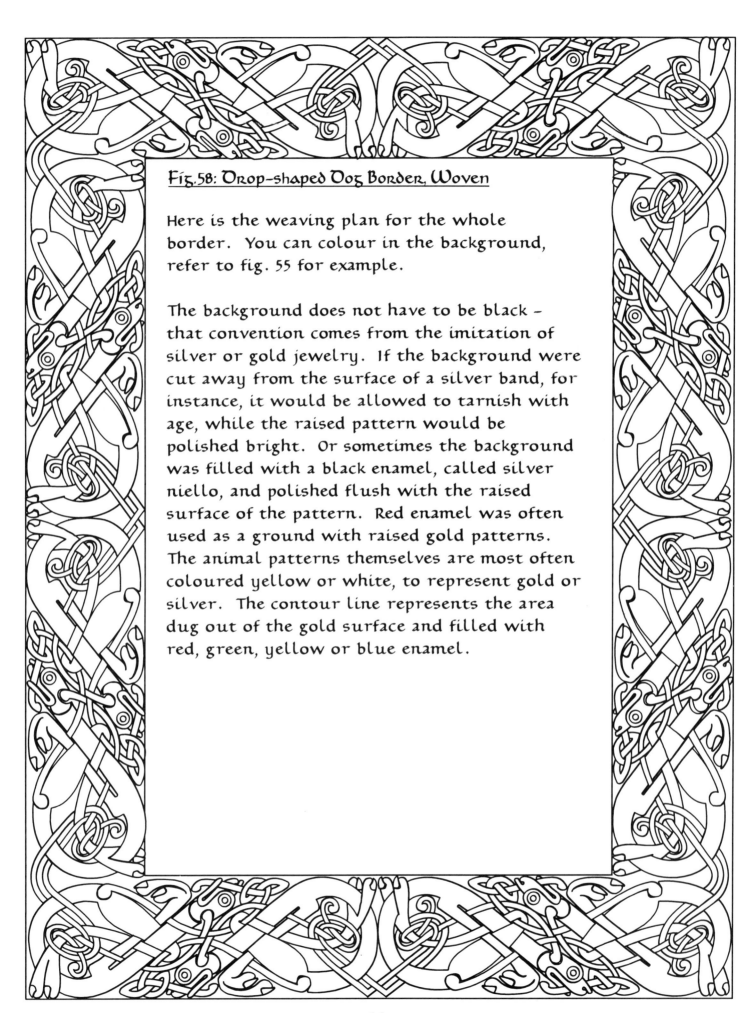

Fig.58: Drop-shaped Dog Border, Woven

Here is the weaving plan for the whole border. You can colour in the background, refer to fig. 55 for example.

The background does not have to be black – that convention comes from the imitation of silver or gold jewelry. If the background were cut away from the surface of a silver band, for instance, it would be allowed to tarnish with age, while the raised pattern would be polished bright. Or sometimes the background was filled with a black enamel, called silver niello, and polished flush with the raised surface of the pattern. Red enamel was often used as a ground with raised gold patterns. The animal patterns themselves are most often coloured yellow or white, to represent gold or silver. The contour line represents the area dug out of the gold surface and filled with red, green, yellow or blue enamel.

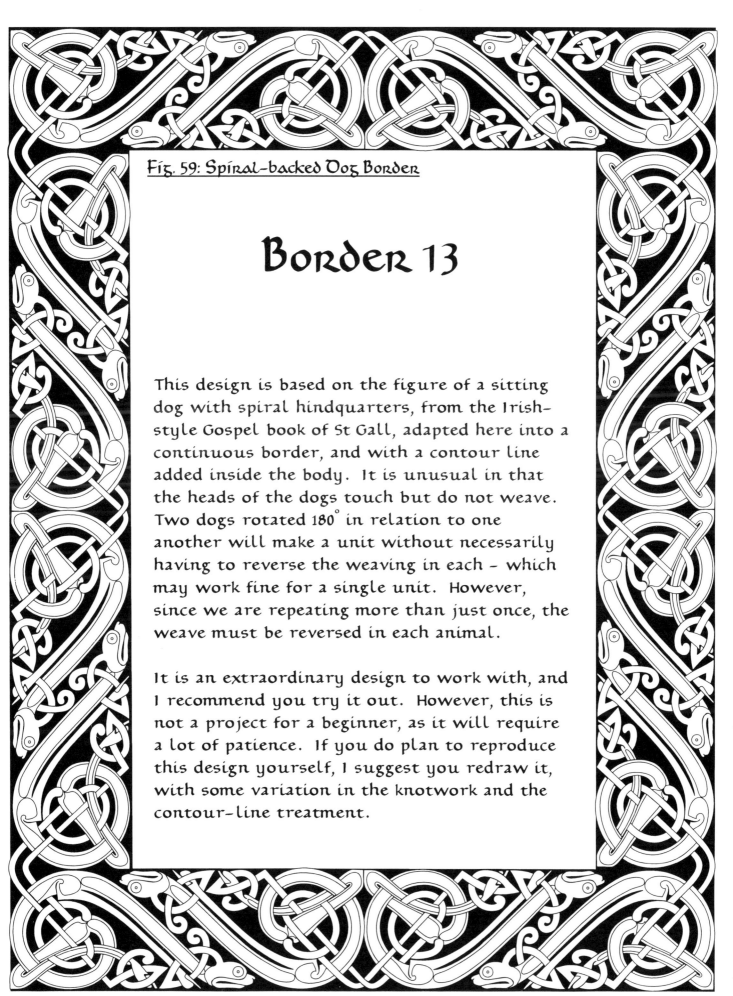

Border 13

This design is based on the figure of a sitting dog with spiral hindquarters, from the Irish-style Gospel book of St Gall, adapted here into a continuous border, and with a contour line added inside the body. It is unusual in that the heads of the dogs touch but do not weave. Two dogs rotated 180° in relation to one another will make a unit without necessarily having to reverse the weaving in each – which may work fine for a single unit. However, since we are repeating more than just once, the weave must be reversed in each animal.

It is an extraordinary design to work with, and I recommend you try it out. However, this is not a project for a beginner, as it will require a lot of patience. If you do plan to reproduce this design yourself, I suggest you redraw it, with some variation in the knotwork and the contour-line treatment.

Fig.60: Spiral-backed Dog Border

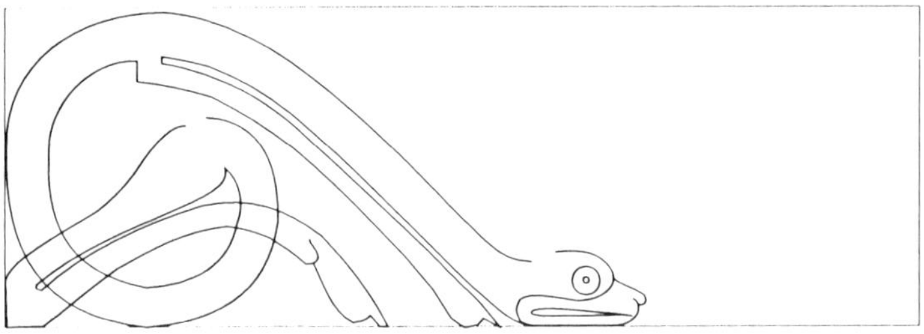

a   Dog with spiral back.

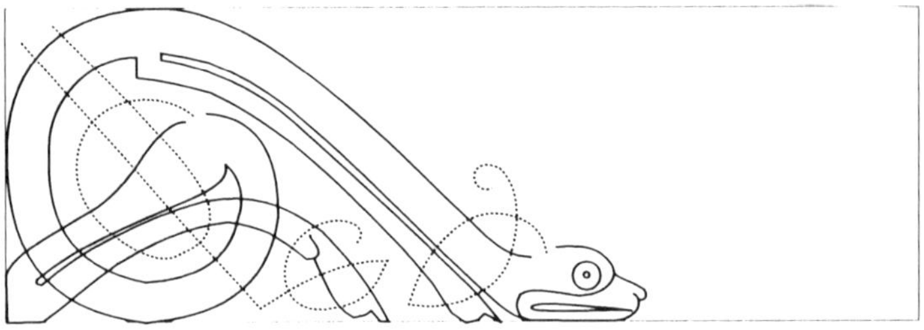

b   Add ear and tail, centre lines pencilled in.

c   Ear and tail lines, outlined.

d   Line plan for stencil pattern below, e.

e

Fig.61: Spiral-backed Dog Border, Layout 2

a   Line plan, one dog rotated, single unit.

b   Tracing stencil plan, from line plan.

c   Line plan, with contour lines.

d   The dogs are woven in opposite directions.

Fig. 62: Spiral-backed Dog Border

a   At the corners, the tails are uncrossed.

b   The dogs are woven in opposite directions in each half of the single unit.

c   In tracing, one woven unit may be rotated and then flipped back-to-back to make a four-dog unit.

d   The tails may be woven continuously between one three-square unit and the next in a six-square strip. But remember, you must cross them here, to avoid orphaning a strand in the knot of the tails.

a

b

c

d

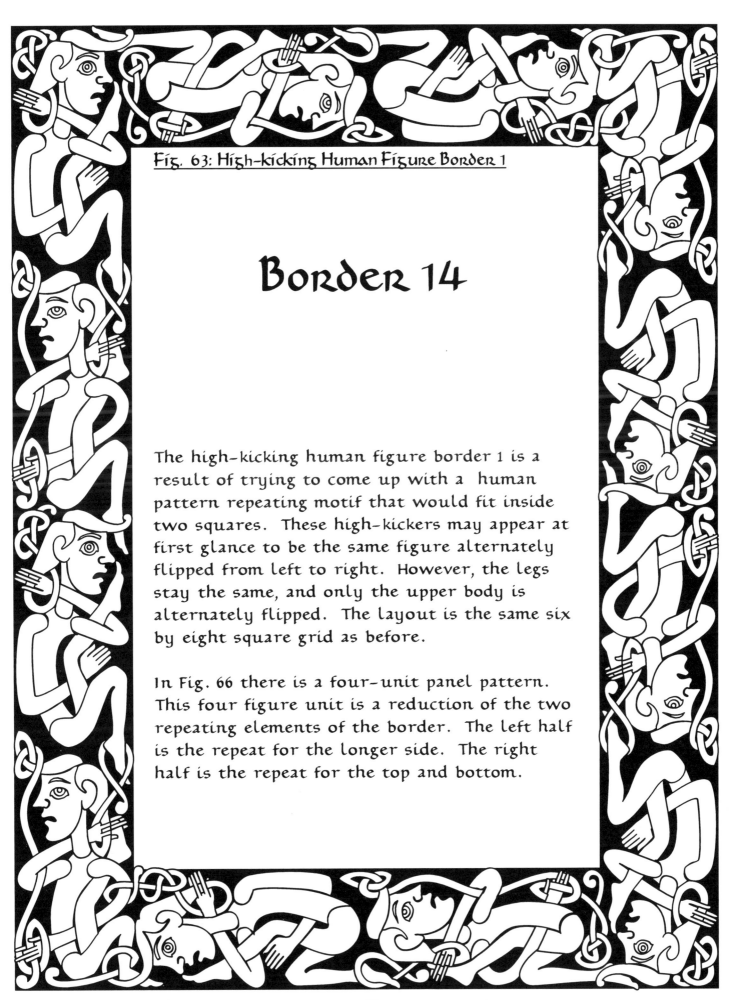

Fig. 63: High-kicking Human Figure Border 1

Border 14

The high-kicking human figure border 1 is a
result of trying to come up with a human
pattern repeating motif that would fit inside
two squares. These high-kickers may appear at
first glance to be the same figure alternately
flipped from left to right. However, the legs
stay the same, and only the upper body is
alternately flipped. The layout is the same six
by eight square grid as before.

In Fig. 66 there is a four-unit panel pattern.
This four figure unit is a reduction of the two
repeating elements of the border. The left half
is the repeat for the longer side. The right
half is the repeat for the top and bottom.

Fig. 64: Layout for Longer Sides

a
line plan for
first figure of
repeating pair
on longer
side.

This pair of
figures should
be traced
into position,
and the
knotwork
added
afterwards,
to allow for
adjustments.

The figures
may be
repeated to fill
the border, two
pairs to each
longer side.
The figures are
rotated 180°
from one side
to the other.

b
line plan for
second figure
of repeating
pair on
longer side.

Adjustments will be made to make the foot fit
inside the frame at the upper or lower edges.

Fig. 65: Line Plan for shorter sides

a
line plan for
first figure of
repeating pair
on shorter
side.

b
line plan for
second figure
of repeating
pair on
shorter side.

A pair of figures at the top and bottom is
sandwiched between the two longer sides.

The figures are traced into position and knots
added after.

Fig. 66: Line Plan for High-kickers Border 1

The figures have been traced and filling knots added. To finish the design, trace the weaving off this plan with a pencil. Transfer the tracing and ink over the pencil lines.

Tip: Always trace the weaving off your line plan so you can reuse it, e.g. for a matching border, woven in the opposite direction.

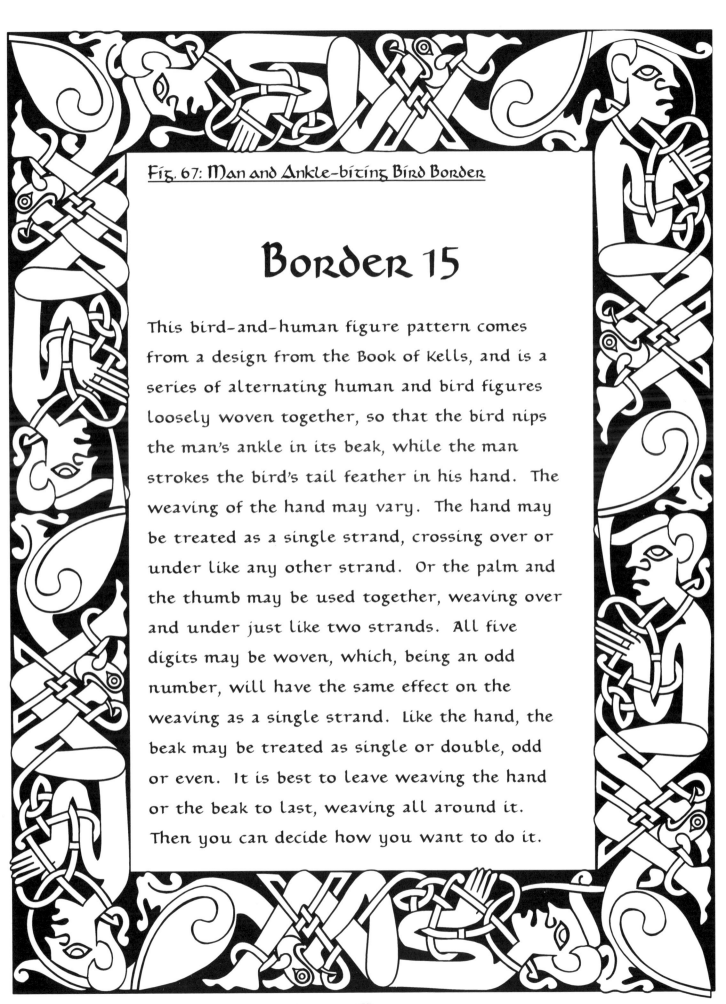

Fig. 67: Man and Ankle-biting Bird Border

Border 15

This bird-and-human figure pattern comes from a design from the Book of Kells, and is a series of alternating human and bird figures loosely woven together, so that the bird nips the man's ankle in its beak, while the man strokes the bird's tail feather in his hand. The weaving of the hand may vary. The hand may be treated as a single strand, crossing over or under like any other strand. Or the palm and the thumb may be used together, weaving over and under just like two strands. All five digits may be woven, which, being an odd number, will have the same effect on the weaving as a single strand. Like the hand, the beak may be treated as single or double, odd or even. It is best to leave weaving the hand or the beak to last, weaving all around it. Then you can decide how you want to do it.

Fig. 68: Man and Ankle-biting Bird Border, Layout 1

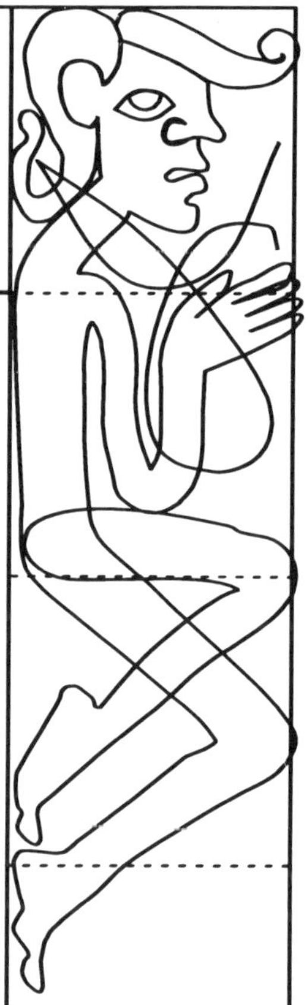

The layout for this border moves away from the three-square basis of most of the borders so far. Here the repeating unit is based on four units instead of three.

With this arrangement, the long sides will hold two units, running the full length of the frame. Sandwiched between these two long sides, four units remain on the top and the bottom edges.

a   Human figure, line sketch.

b   Bird figure, line sketch.

c   Combination of both figures.

a

b

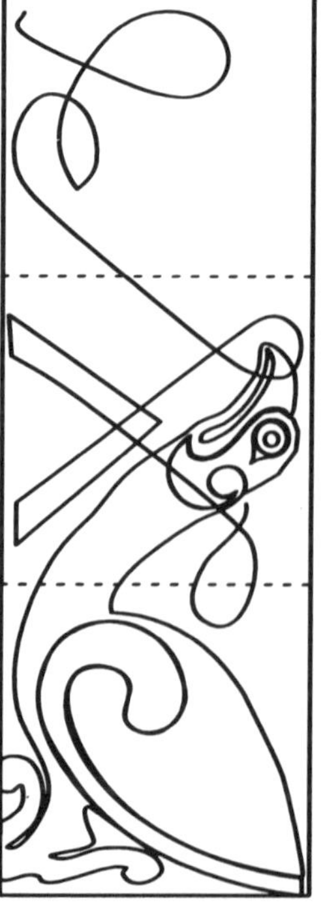

c

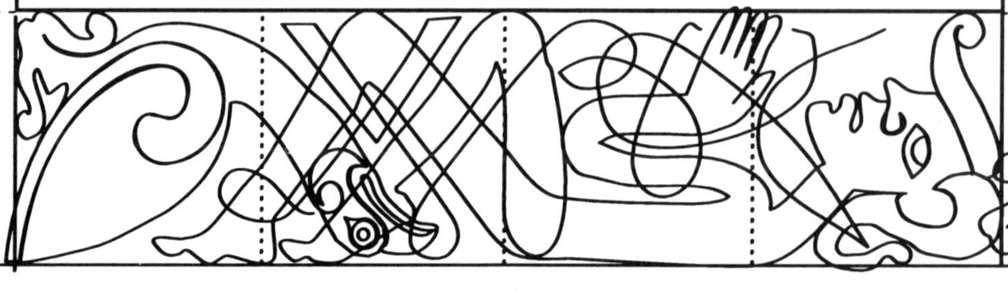

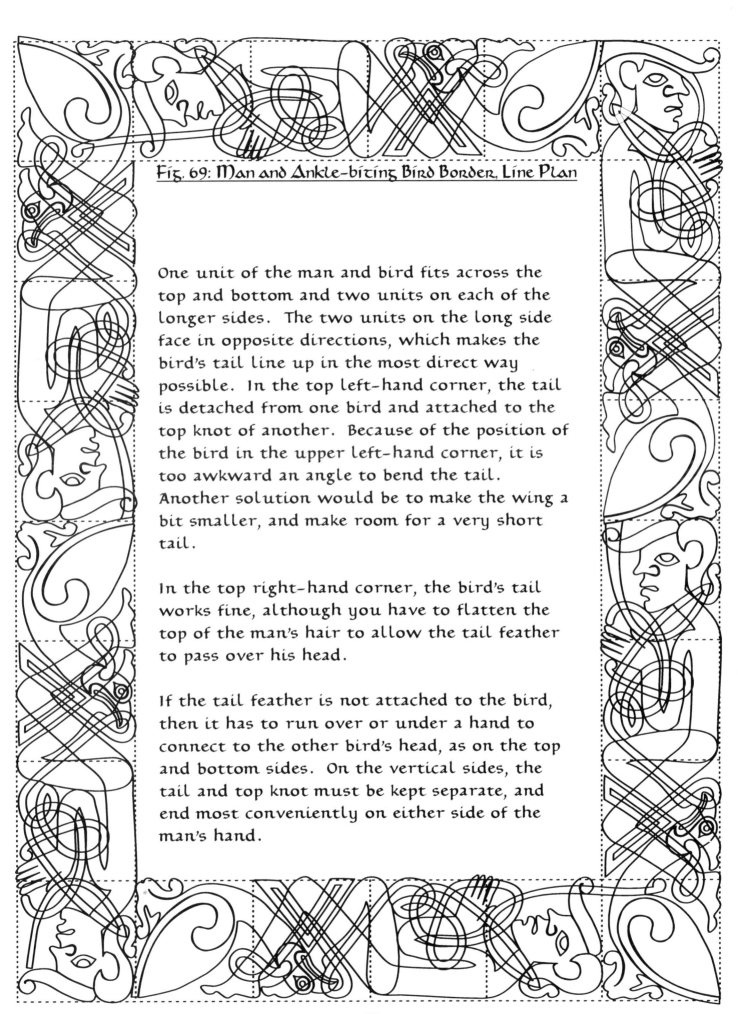

Fig. 69: Man and Ankle-biting Bird Border, Line Plan

One unit of the man and bird fits across the top and bottom and two units on each of the longer sides. The two units on the long side face in opposite directions, which makes the bird's tail line up in the most direct way possible. In the top left-hand corner, the tail is detached from one bird and attached to the top knot of another. Because of the position of the bird in the upper left-hand corner, it is too awkward an angle to bend the tail. Another solution would be to make the wing a bit smaller, and make room for a very short tail.

In the top right-hand corner, the bird's tail works fine, although you have to flatten the top of the man's hair to allow the tail feather to pass over his head.

If the tail feather is not attached to the bird, then it has to run over or under a hand to connect to the other bird's head, as on the top and bottom sides. On the vertical sides, the tail and top knot must be kept separate, and end most conveniently on either side of the man's hand.

Fig. 70: Dotted-Line Weaving Exercise

You can use this dotted line plan as an exercise in weaving the pattern. Using a sharp pencil, start in the upper left corner, and weave over and under each intersection from there. If in doubt, refer to the previous figures.

Use a sharp pencil so that if you make a mistake in the weaving, you can erase it. Only if you have a lot of previous experience drawing knotwork should you try to weave the pattern without pencilling it first. Ink it only after you have pencilled it, and compared it with the solid line weaving on the other side to make sure you have woven it correctly, particularly at the corners, where one side connects to another.

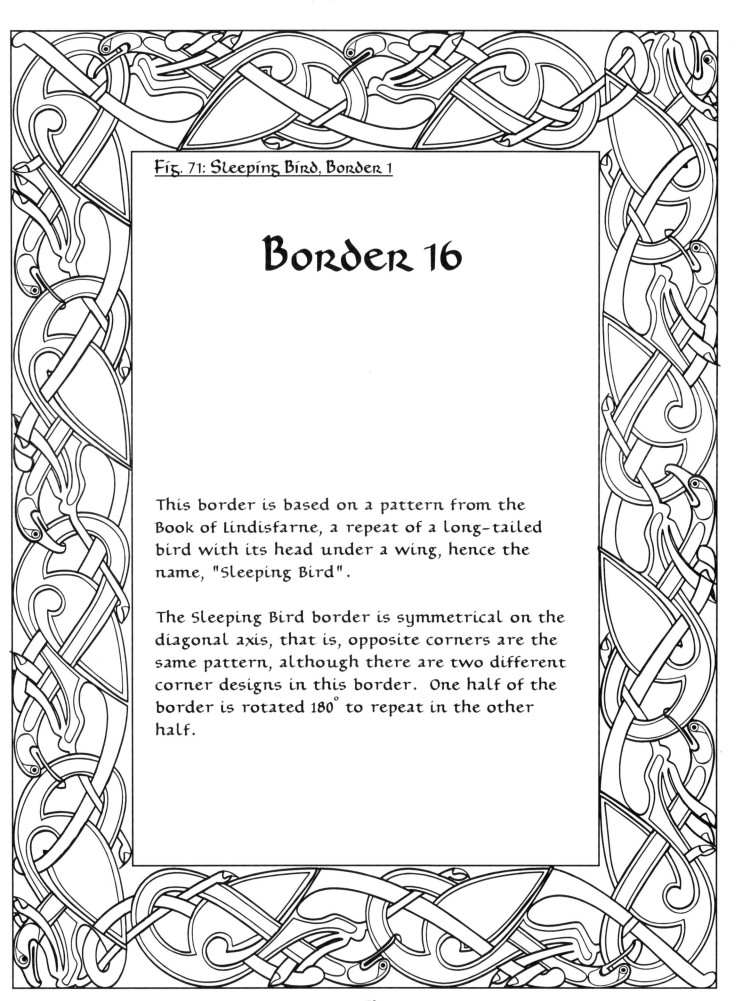

Border 16

This border is based on a pattern from the Book of Lindisfarne, a repeat of a long-tailed bird with its head under a wing, hence the name, "Sleeping Bird".

The Sleeping Bird border is symmetrical on the diagonal axis, that is, opposite corners are the same pattern, although there are two different corner designs in this border. One half of the border is rotated 180° to repeat in the other half.

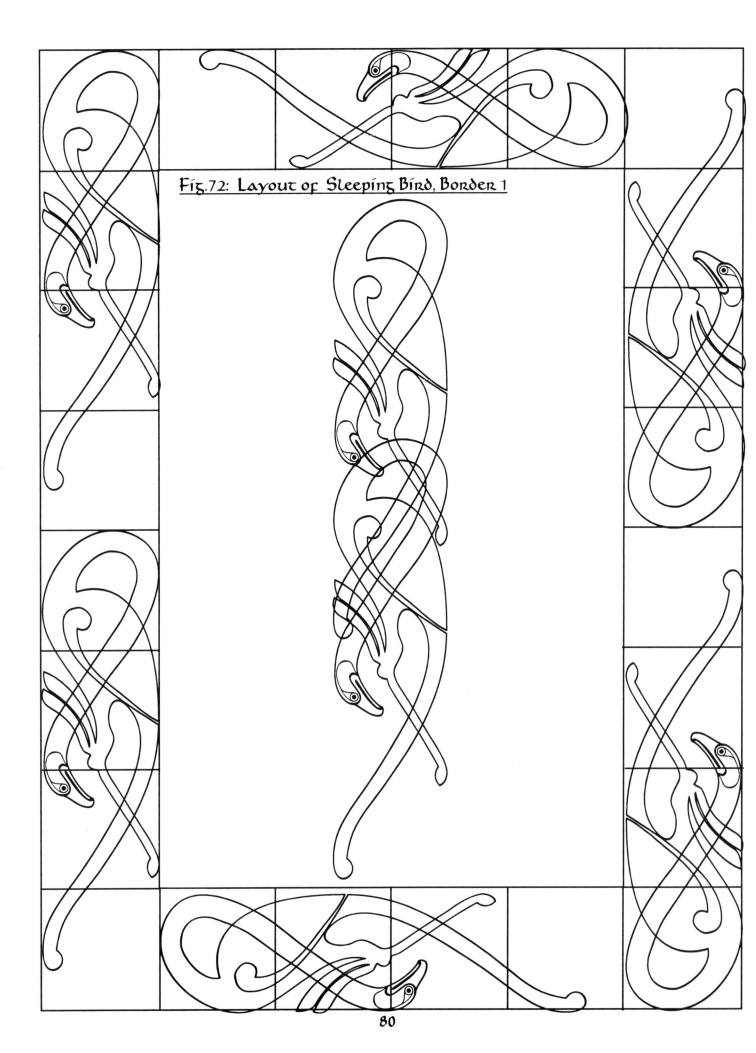

Fig.72: Layout of Sleeping Bird, Border 1

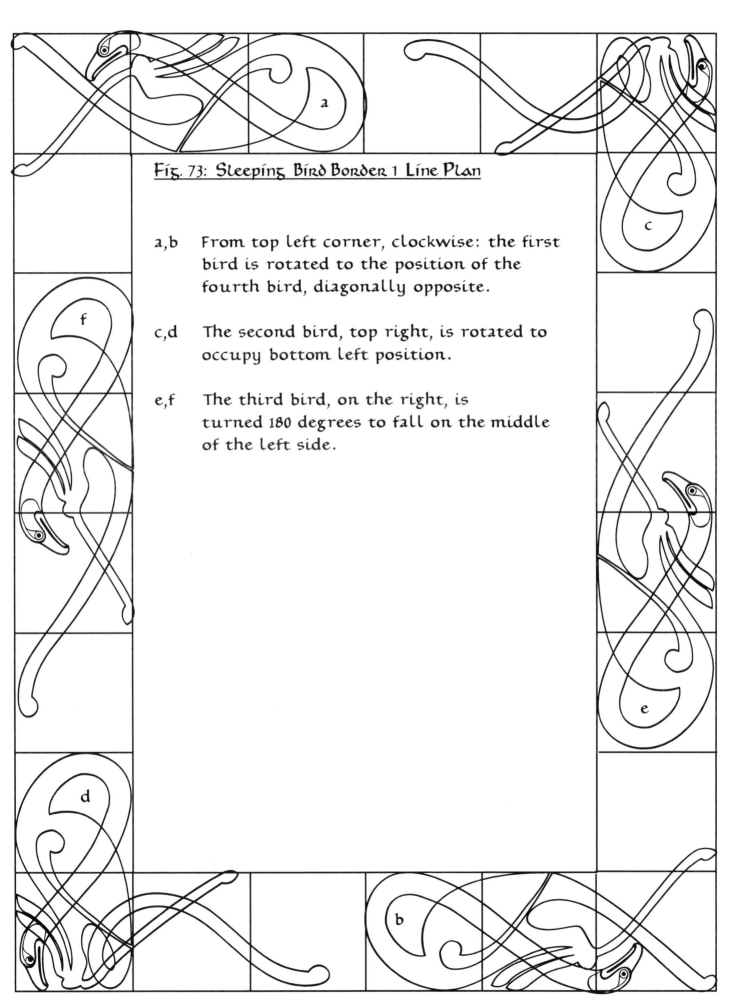

Fig. 73: Sleeping Bird Border 1 Line Plan

a,b   From top left corner, clockwise: the first bird is rotated to the position of the fourth bird, diagonally opposite.

c,d   The second bird, top right, is rotated to occupy bottom left position.

e,f   The third bird, on the right, is turned 180 degrees to fall on the middle of the left side.

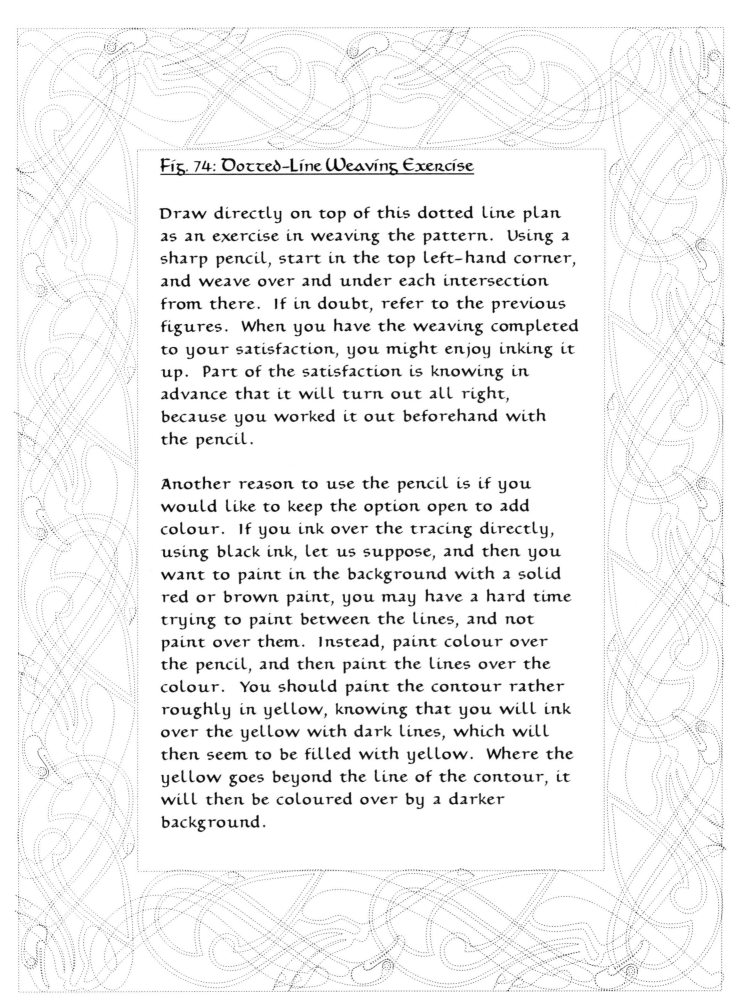

Fig. 74: Dotted-Line Weaving Exercise

Draw directly on top of this dotted line plan as an exercise in weaving the pattern. Using a sharp pencil, start in the top left-hand corner, and weave over and under each intersection from there. If in doubt, refer to the previous figures. When you have the weaving completed to your satisfaction, you might enjoy inking it up. Part of the satisfaction is knowing in advance that it will turn out all right, because you worked it out beforehand with the pencil.

Another reason to use the pencil is if you would like to keep the option open to add colour. If you ink over the tracing directly, using black ink, let us suppose, and then you want to paint in the background with a solid red or brown paint, you may have a hard time trying to paint between the lines, and not paint over them. Instead, paint colour over the pencil, and then paint the lines over the colour. You should paint the contour rather roughly in yellow, knowing that you will ink over the yellow with dark lines, which will then seem to be filled with yellow. Where the yellow goes beyond the line of the contour, it will then be coloured over by a darker background.

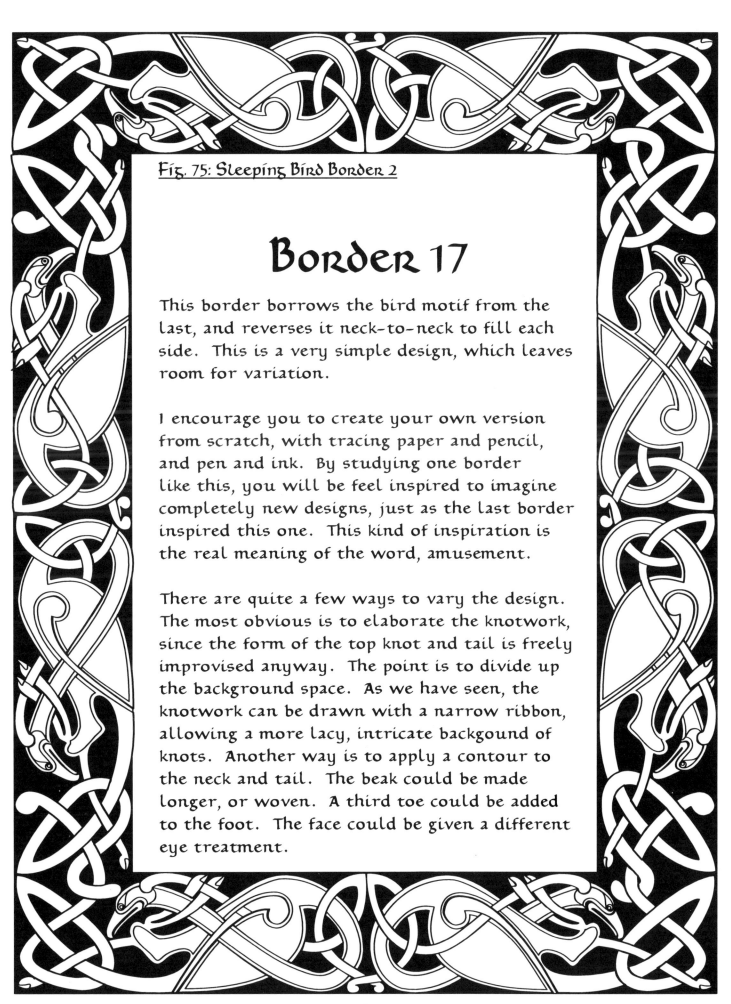

Border 17

This border borrows the bird motif from the last, and reverses it neck-to-neck to fill each side. This is a very simple design, which leaves room for variation.

I encourage you to create your own version from scratch, with tracing paper and pencil, and pen and ink. By studying one border like this, you will be feel inspired to imagine completely new designs, just as the last border inspired this one. This kind of inspiration is the real meaning of the word, amusement.

There are quite a few ways to vary the design. The most obvious is to elaborate the knotwork, since the form of the top knot and tail is freely improvised anyway. The point is to divide up the background space. As we have seen, the knotwork can be drawn with a narrow ribbon, allowing a more lacy, intricate backgound of knots. Another way is to apply a contour to the neck and tail. The beak could be made longer, or woven. A third toe could be added to the foot. The face could be given a different eye treatment.

a

Fig. 76: Layout for Sleeping Bird Border 2

a   Line plan for a single unit of the sleeping bird motif.

b   Line plan for strip of two birds.

A single bird takes up three spaces (above, a).

A pair of birds occupy six spaces. There are six spaces between the horizontal strips at the top and the bottom.

b

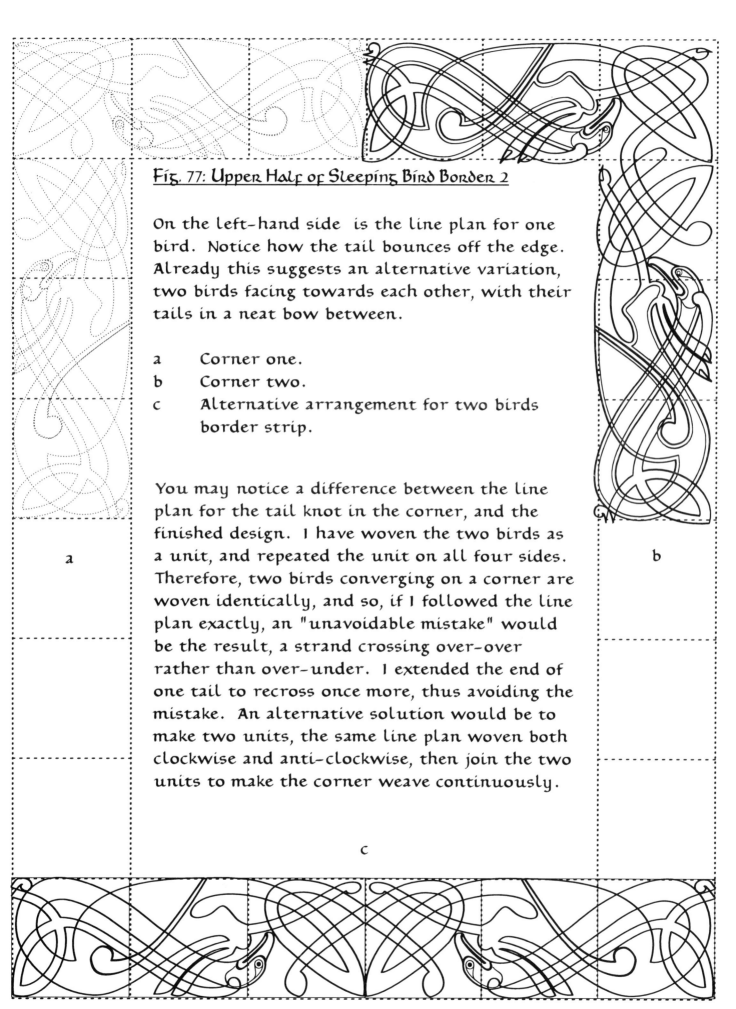

Fig. 77: Upper Half of Sleeping Bird Border 2

On the left-hand side is the line plan for one bird. Notice how the tail bounces off the edge. Already this suggests an alternative variation, two birds facing towards each other, with their tails in a neat bow between.

a   Corner one.
b   Corner two.
c   Alternative arrangement for two birds border strip.

You may notice a difference between the line plan for the tail knot in the corner, and the finished design. I have woven the two birds as a unit, and repeated the unit on all four sides. Therefore, two birds converging on a corner are woven identically, and so, if I followed the line plan exactly, an "unavoidable mistake" would be the result, a strand crossing over-over rather than over-under. I extended the end of one tail to recross once more, thus avoiding the mistake. An alternative solution would be to make two units, the same line plan woven both clockwise and anti-clockwise, then join the two units to make the corner weave continuously.

a

b

c

Fig. 78: Line Plan for Sleeping Bird Border 2

In this plan, we see the lines for the birds ready to be woven, but also the extra lines for the contour line inside the body, from the head to the foot, and around the wing.

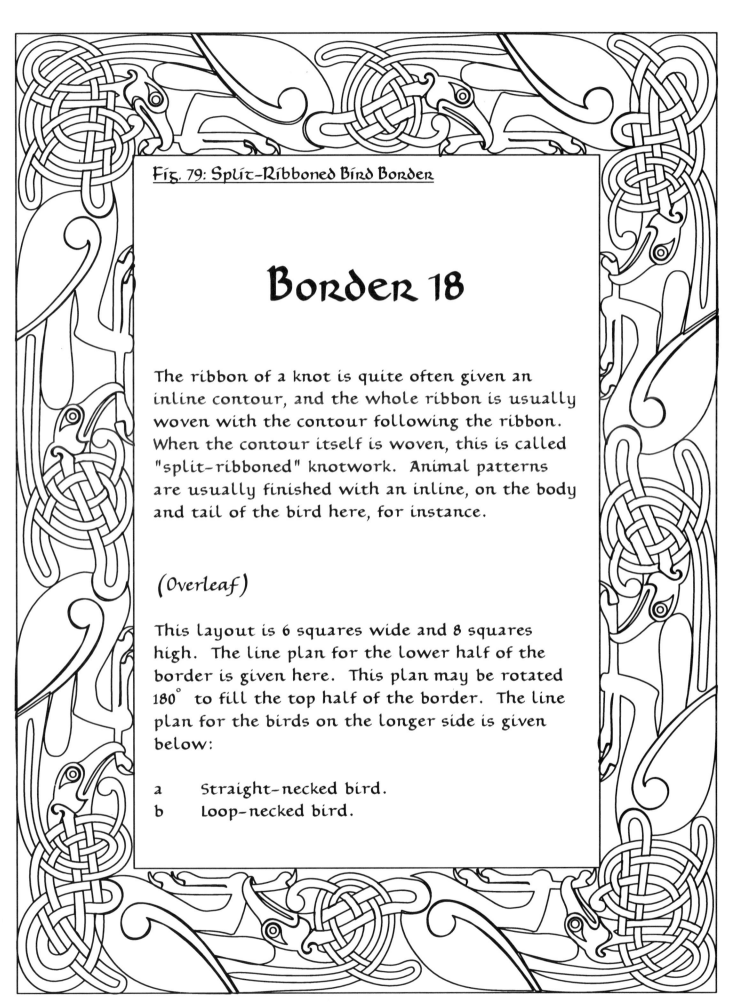

Border 18

The ribbon of a knot is quite often given an inline contour, and the whole ribbon is usually woven with the contour following the ribbon. When the contour itself is woven, this is called "split-ribboned" knotwork. Animal patterns are usually finished with an inline, on the body and tail of the bird here, for instance.

(Overleaf)

This layout is 6 squares wide and 8 squares high. The line plan for the lower half of the border is given here. This plan may be rotated 180° to fill the top half of the border. The line plan for the birds on the longer side is given below:

a   Straight-necked bird.
b   Loop-necked bird.

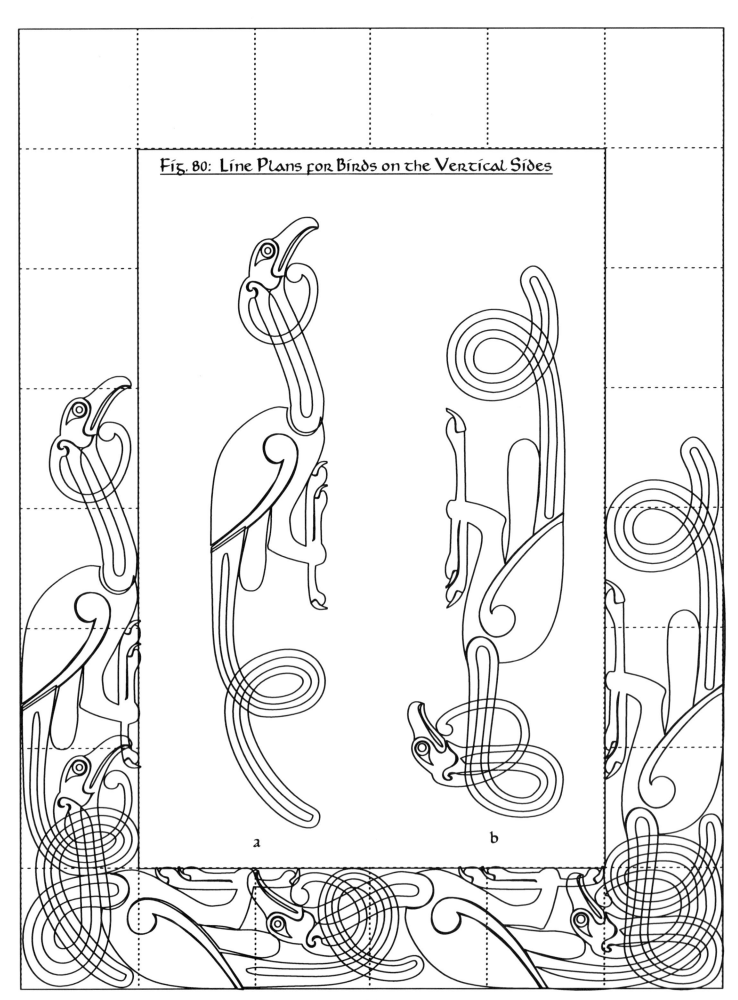

Fig. 80: Line Plans for Birds on the Vertical Sides

a

b

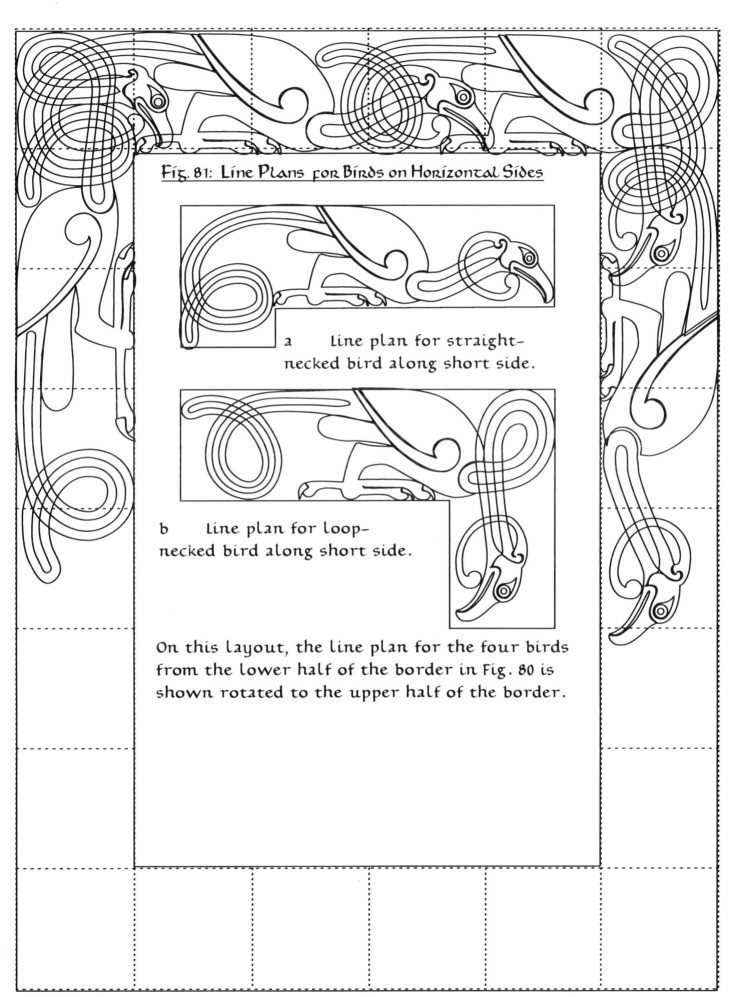

Fig. 81: Line Plans for Birds on Horizontal Sides

a   line plan for straight-
necked bird along short side.

b   line plan for loop-
necked bird along short side.

On this layout, the line plan for the four birds
from the lower half of the border in Fig. 80 is
shown rotated to the upper half of the border.

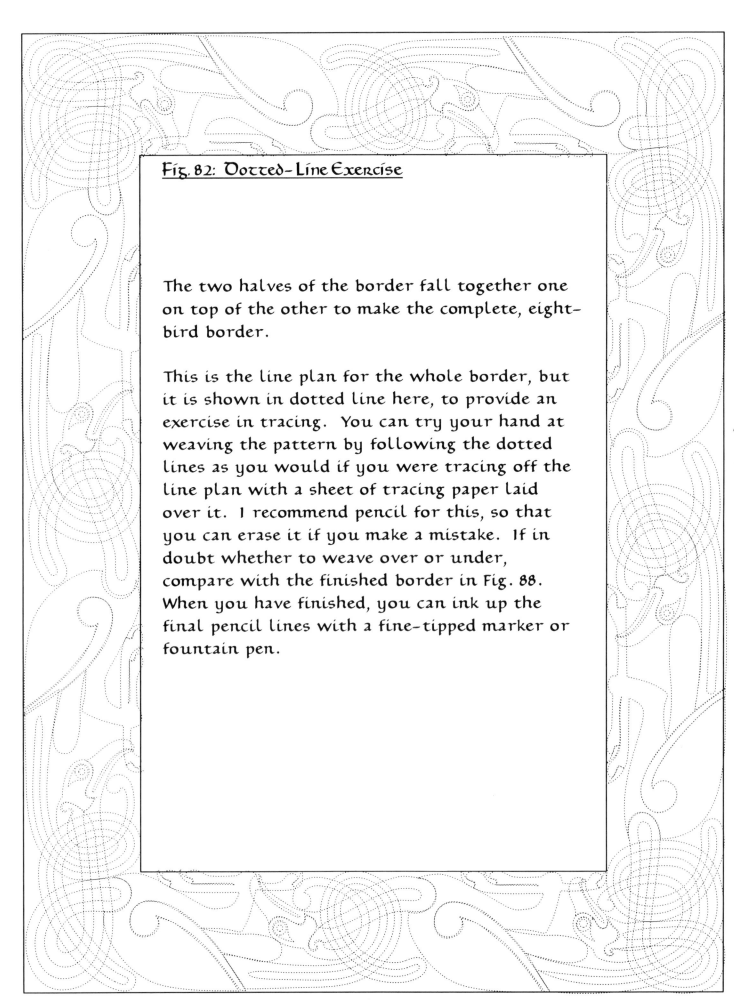

Fig. 82: Dotted-Line Exercise

The two halves of the border fall together one on top of the other to make the complete, eight-bird border.

This is the line plan for the whole border, but it is shown in dotted line here, to provide an exercise in tracing. You can try your hand at weaving the pattern by following the dotted lines as you would if you were tracing off the line plan with a sheet of tracing paper laid over it. I recommend pencil for this, so that you can erase it if you make a mistake. If in doubt whether to weave over or under, compare with the finished border in Fig. 88. When you have finished, you can ink up the final pencil lines with a fine-tipped marker or fountain pen.

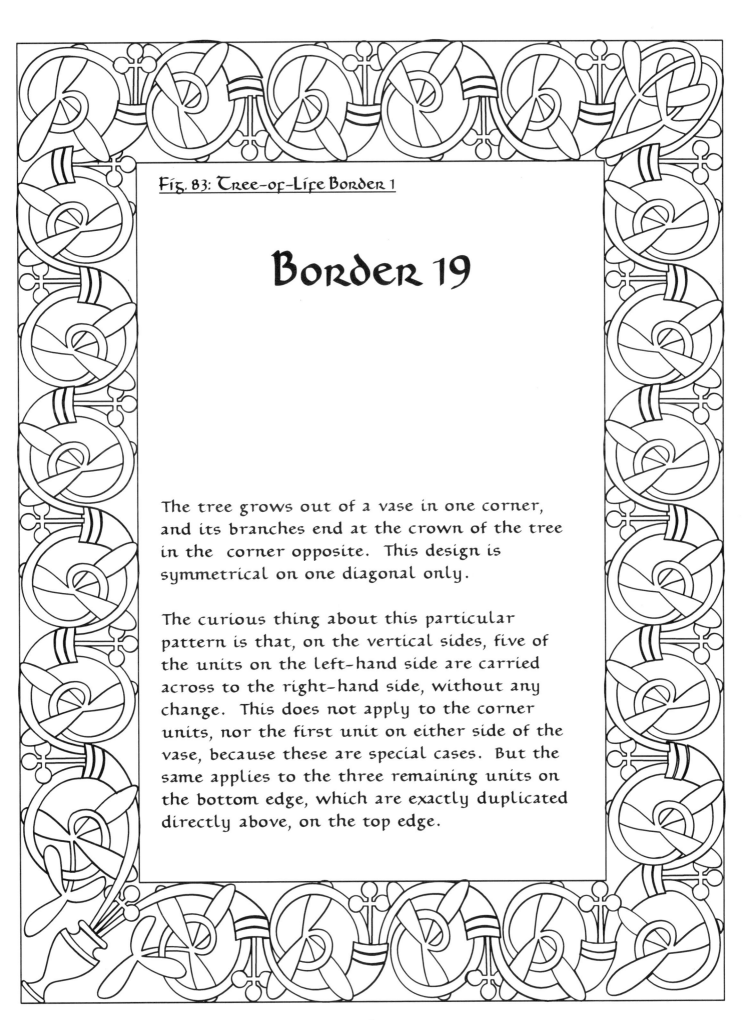

Border 19

The tree grows out of a vase in one corner, and its branches end at the crown of the tree in the corner opposite. This design is symmetrical on one diagonal only.

The curious thing about this particular pattern is that, on the vertical sides, five of the units on the left-hand side are carried across to the right-hand side, without any change. This does not apply to the corner units, nor the first unit on either side of the vase, because these are special cases. But the same applies to the three remaining units on the bottom edge, which are exactly duplicated directly above, on the top edge.

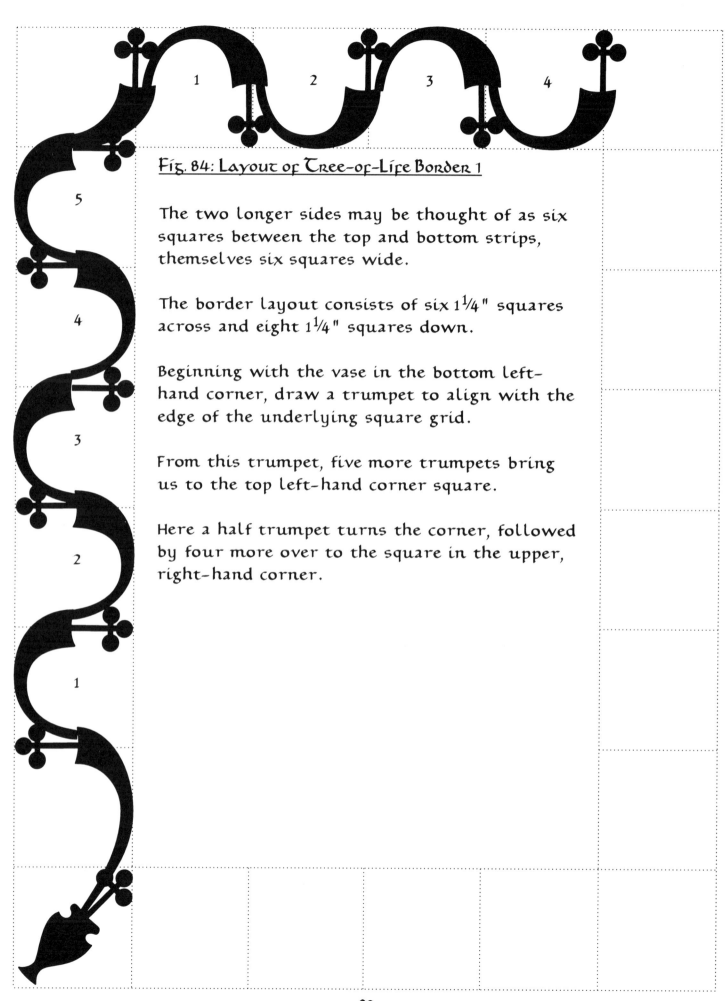

Fig. 84: Layout of Tree-of-Life Border 1

The two longer sides may be thought of as six squares between the top and bottom strips, themselves six squares wide.

The border layout consists of six $1\frac{1}{4}$" squares across and eight $1\frac{1}{4}$" squares down.

Beginning with the vase in the bottom left-hand corner, draw a trumpet to align with the edge of the underlying square grid.

From this trumpet, five more trumpets bring us to the top left-hand corner square.

Here a half trumpet turns the corner, followed by four more over to the square in the upper, right-hand corner.

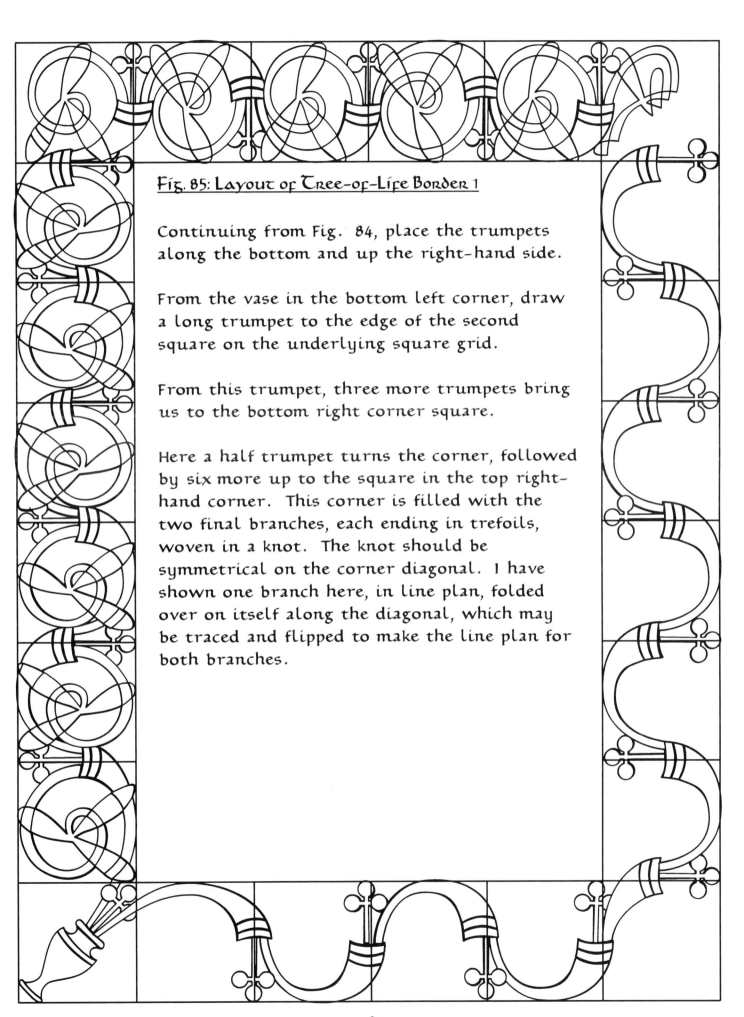

Fig. 85: Layout of Tree-of-Life Border 1

Continuing from Fig. 84, place the trumpets along the bottom and up the right-hand side.

From the vase in the bottom left corner, draw a long trumpet to the edge of the second square on the underlying square grid.

From this trumpet, three more trumpets bring us to the bottom right corner square.

Here a half trumpet turns the corner, followed by six more up to the square in the top right-hand corner. This corner is filled with the two final branches, each ending in trefoils, woven in a knot. The knot should be symmetrical on the corner diagonal. I have shown one branch here, in line plan, folded over on itself along the diagonal, which may be traced and flipped to make the line plan for both branches.

Fig. 86: Line Plan for Tree-of-Life Border 1

The weaving of the pattern at Fig. 83, above, is traced off a line plan such as this.

Remember, when you are designing your own Celtic border, and you have traced it up to this stage in pencil, think carefully before you rush ahead to ink over the line plan.

Rather than inking over it directly, trace the weaving off the line plan. There is always more than one way to weave the final design from one plan. By saving your line pattern, you can try out other variations.

Also, sometimes the weaving will not work out because of a fundamental flaw in the underlying line plan, which you could not have foreseen. Then you need to go back to the line plan, and adjust it. For instance, in this design I first tried it with four leaves on each spiral, but when I went to weave it, I found it would invariably come out wrong. After much trial and error, I discovered that by using three leaves instead of four, it would weave perfectly. I saved myself hours of work just by keeping a copy of the line plan.

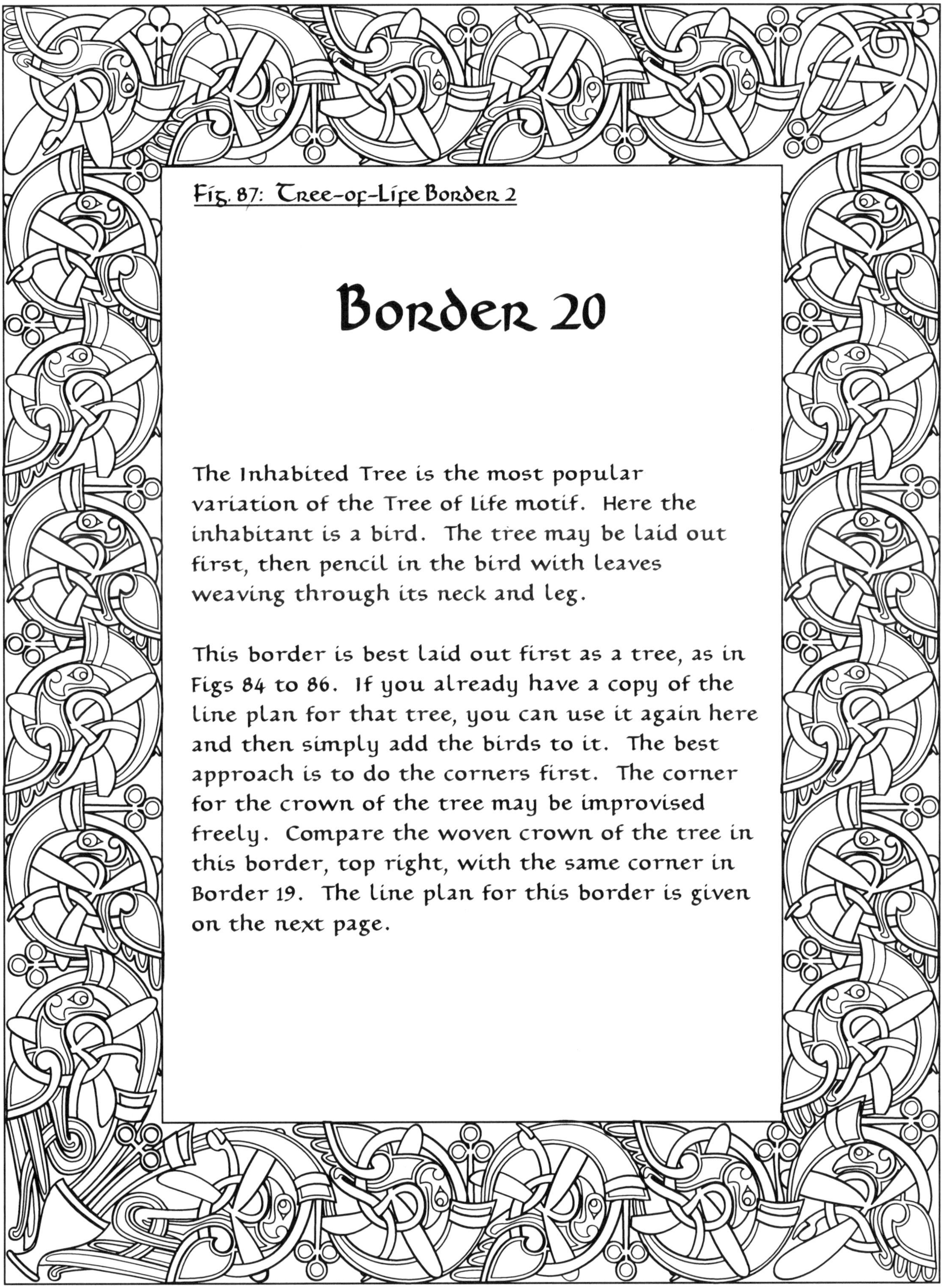

Fig. 87: Tree-of-Life Border 2

Border 20

The Inhabited Tree is the most popular variation of the Tree of Life motif. Here the inhabitant is a bird. The tree may be laid out first, then pencil in the bird with leaves weaving through its neck and leg.

This border is best laid out first as a tree, as in Figs 84 to 86. If you already have a copy of the line plan for that tree, you can use it again here and then simply add the birds to it. The best approach is to do the corners first. The corner for the crown of the tree may be improvised freely. Compare the woven crown of the tree in this border, top right, with the same corner in Border 19. The line plan for this border is given on the next page.

Fig. 88: Line Plan for Tree-of-Life Border 2

This repeat unit fills two squares. We need three corners, one for upper left and lower right; one pot, below left; and one woven crown, top right.